Super sweets & puddings

Myrtle Lindlaw

COLLINS

Glasgow & London

© General Foods 1974
First published 1974
ISBN 0 00 435101 0 (Cased)
ISBN 0 00 435102 3 (Paperback)

Designed and edited by Youé and Spooner Ltd.
Photography by Rex Bamber

Printed and bound in Great Britain
by William Collins Sons & Co. Ltd.

*Front cover: Raspberry mille feuilles (page 91),
Midsummer pie (page 25), Jelly jewels (page 58),
Mandarin flan (page 30) and Dream slices (page 67)*

Back cover: Christmas pudding (page 18)

Contents

A question my mother often used to ask when we were children was: "What shall we have for pudding?" We were very fond of puddings and many of our well tried family favourites are contained in this book. I hope that you will be reminded of recipes you used to enjoy and perhaps have half forgotten over the years and that, when you browse through the pages and see the pictures, you will be tempted to make them once more.

As well as the more familiar recipes, you will find extravagant desserts which are gorgeous for treats and when entertaining special guests. The busy mum and working wife will find the Quick 'n' easy puddings chapter an invaluable aid when she turns to her store cupboard to produce a distinctive end to an impromptu meal.

It has been great fun compiling and testing these recipes for you and I hope that you and your family will enjoy the results. I would particularly like to thank my friends and colleagues at General Foods Ltd. for the tremendous help and encouragement they have given me in the preparation of this book.

Myrtle Lindlaw

Basic techniques & metrication

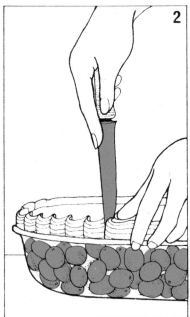

To knock up (see fig 1)
A decorative way of finishing a cut pastry edge as on a pie. Press the back of the index finger of the left hand on the top of the pastry and, using a sharp knife, flake the edge of the pastry parallel to the dish.

To scallop (see fig 2)
To flute the edges of a pie. With the right hand, draw a knife sharply upwards and inwards across the edge of the pastry, holding the pastry with the thumb of the left hand and pushing out slightly to form scallops. Traditionally, savoury pies have large scallops, fruit pies small ones.

To bake blind (see figs 3 and 4)
Prick the pastry, cover with a piece of muslin kept for the purpose or a piece of greaseproof paper and fill with crusts of bread or haricot beans, which can be used time and again. Bake as directed in the recipe and remove the crusts or beans towards the end of baking by lifting out the muslin or greaseproof paper. Complete the baking.

To rub in
A method of incorporating fat into flour as used in pastry or plain cake mixtures. Pick up small handfuls of fat and flour and rub the thumbs lightly across the fingers, allowing the mixture to drop back into the mixing bowl. Continue until the fat is well distributed and the mixture looks like fresh breadcrumbs.

To fold in
To combine an ingredient such as flour with an aerated ingredient such as whisked egg whites. Do this carefully using a metal spoon. Cut through the mixture vertically and lift it lightly to lie on the top. Repeat until the ingredients are just incorporated.

To cream
To beat fat and sugar together until they are light and creamy. Use a wide-topped bowl and a wooden spoon or, for large quantities, cream with your hand.

To infuse
To flavour a liquid by heating it slowly to boiling point with a flavouring such as thinly pared lemon rind, orange rind or vanilla pod. Strain before use.

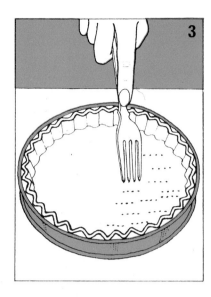

To simmer
To cook at just below boiling point. Only an occasional bubble should rise to the surface when a pudding or liquid is simmering.

To separate eggs
Break the egg on to a saucer, invert an egg cup on the yolk and drain off the white into a basin. Alternatively, break the egg in two over a basin, hold half shells like two cups and gently tip the yolk from one half shell to the other. The white will gradually drop into the basin.

To whisk cream
Use double cream or whipping cream. More volume is obtained if the cream is chilled. Add sugar or flavouring as required and whisk steadily, watching carefully to catch the cream at the desired consistency, as over-whisked cream cannot be remedied.

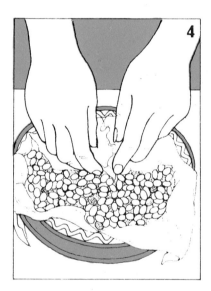

To unmould jelly
Have ready the serving dish and a large bowl of water slightly hotter than the hand can bear. Working quickly, immerse the mould completely in the water for a second (china or plastic moulds need longer). Dry the mould, then shake slightly to loosen the jelly. Sprinkle the centre of the serving dish with water, invert on the mould, then invert the plate and mould together. Lift off the mould carefully and gently slide the jelly to the centre of the dish.

To unmould blancmange
Have ready a serving dish with the centre sprinkled with water. Gently ease the blancmange away from the edge of the mould, using the fingertips. Invert the mould on to the serving dish as centrally as possible. Gripping the edges of the plate and top of the mould firmly, shake sharply up and down. This should release the blancmange. Lift off the mould carefully. The wet plate will now enable you to gently slide the blancmange to the centre.

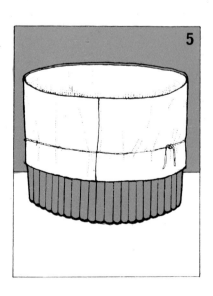

To unmould ice cream
Hold the mould or ice tray under the cold tap and let it run for a few minutes to loosen the ice cream. Turn on to a dish.

To prepare a soufflé dish (see fig 5)
Tie round it a double band of foil or greaseproof paper. The band should fit tightly and stand 2 inches (5cm) above the rim of the dish.

To prepare a cake for icing
Brush off loose crumbs. Spread on a very thin layer of icing to seal the remaining crumbs to the cake before swirling on the rest of the icing.

Temperatures

Oven temperature equivalents

	Gas	Electric	
	Mark	Fahrenheit	Celsius
very cool	$\frac{1}{4}$	225	110
cool	$\frac{1}{2}$	250	130
very slow	1	275	140
slow	2	300	150
very moderate	3	325	170
moderate	4	350	180
moderately hot	5	375	190
fairly hot	6	400	200
hot	7	425	220
very hot	8	450	230
extremely hot	9	475	240

These oven heats and settings are meant as a guide to help you when using recipes that are prepared especially for a gas or electric cooker or are rather vague and give just an indication of oven heat, for example, cook in a moderate oven.

Use this chart in conjunction with the recipe book supplied with your cooker.

Weights and metric equivalents

$\frac{1}{2}$oz converts to	15 grams
1oz ,, ,,	25 grams
2oz ,, ,,	50 grams
3oz ,, ,,	75 grams
4oz ,, ,,	100 grams
5oz ,, ,,	150 grams
6oz ,, ,,	175 grams
7oz ,, ,,	200 grams
8oz ,, ,,	225 grams
9oz ,, ,,	250 grams
10oz ,, ,,	275 grams
11oz ,, ,,	300 grams
12oz ,, ,,	350 grams
13oz ,, ,,	375 grams
14oz ,, ,,	400 grams
15oz ,, ,,	425 grams
16oz ,, ,,	450 grams

1 pint = 6dl
$\frac{3}{4}$ pint = $4\frac{1}{2}$dl
$\frac{1}{2}$ pint = 3dl
$\frac{1}{4}$ pint = $1\frac{1}{2}$dl

This book incorporates both imperial and metric measurements, so that the recipes are readily understood in both measures.

The Metrication Board recognises that an exact conversion of 1 ounce gives the very awkward figure of 28·35 grams, so it recommends using 25 grams as the base for 1 ounce.

We have found the table on the left a good guide in converting recipes. You will notice that this guide deviates slightly from the Metrication Board's general rule, but we have found, when converting the recipes in this book, it helps to keep the baking tins and baking times constant for both the imperial and metric recipe. Gram has been abbreviated throughout to g.

The can sizes when given are those as currently stated on the can, i.e. $15\frac{1}{2}$oz (439g) or $14\frac{1}{4}$oz (404g).

Liquid measures
Domestic recipes rarely use 1 litre of liquid, which is equivalent to $1\frac{3}{4}$ pints. Metric measuring jugs will be marked in decilitres, abbreviated dl, and the conversions are shown on the left.

For smaller quantities millilitres may be used and these have been abbreviated to ml.

Decorations and garnishes

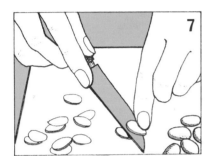

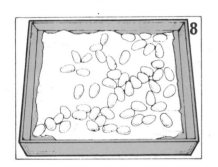

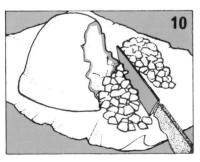

Hazelnuts
To skin: put the nuts in a single layer on a baking sheet and warm thoroughly in a very moderate oven, Gas Mark 3; 325°F (170°C) for 7–10 minutes, or grill gently until quite warm. The skins will then rub away.

Pistachio nuts
To skin: put the nuts into a small saucepan of cold water to which has been added a pinch of bicarbonate of soda. Bring to the boil, strain and put the nuts in cold water. Rub the nuts between the thumb and first finger to remove the skin. Pistachio nuts are usually chopped very finely before use.

Almonds
To blanch: put into a saucepan of cold water, bring to the boil, strain and put into cold water. Rub the nuts between the thumb and first finger to remove the skin. Dry.

To slither (see fig 6): put the blanched almonds on a board and, using a sharp knife, cut them into shreds the long way of the nut. If the almonds are too brittle to cut easily, cover them with boiling water for 30 seconds, then shred them.

To flake (see fig 7): cut the nut thinly the shallow way of the nut, split in half, then split each half through. Again, brittle nuts can be softened in boiling water before flaking.

To brown (see fig 8): put blanched whole, chopped, slithered or flaked almonds on to a foil-lined shallow baking tin and put to brown in a very moderate oven, Gas Mark 3; 325°F (170°C), shaking frequently.

Angelica (see fig 9)
When bought in small, see-through packs, it is ready for use. Just cut into strips about $\frac{1}{4}$ inch (·5cm) wide, then cut these strips across diagonally to produce the traditional diamond shape for angelica garnish. When it is bought by the stick or $\frac{1}{2}$lb (225g), cut off sufficient for your purpose, wash in hot water to remove the crystallised sugar and proceed as above.

Chopped jelly (see fig 10)
Have extra stiff jelly by making it up to just $\frac{3}{4}$ pint (4$\frac{1}{2}$dl) with water. When set, turn on to wet greaseproof paper, sprinkle the jelly with cold water and chop with a sharp knife. Sprinkle with cold water before use—this improves the sparkle of the jelly.

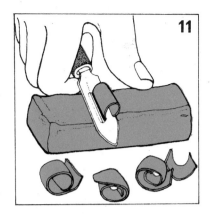

Chocolate

To melt: put the chocolate on a plate over a pan of hot water and leave to melt. Remember that melted chocolate tends to hold its shape till stirred.

To make chocolate curls (see fig 11): soften the chocolate very slightly—the temperature of a gas oven with just the pilot light on is perfect—but do not put over direct heat or hot water. Shave with a potato peeler or knife frequently dipped in hot water.

Desiccated coconut

To colour: dilute a few drops of food colouring in 1 teaspoon milk or water, add 3–4 level tablespoons desiccated coconut and toss with a fork till evenly tinted.

To toast: spread the desiccated coconut on foil on a baking tray. Toast in a very moderate oven, Gas Mark 3; 325°F (170°C), stirring often for about 10 minutes, or until lightly browned. It can be toasted more quickly under the grill but take care not to scorch it.

Piped decorations (see fig 12)
To make these you will need:

A forcing bag
These are now mostly nylon or a plastic substance that is easily washed and quickly dried.

Icing or large pipes
These can be bought in many different shapes and sizes. The most used are:

Icing pipes
Tala No. 8, rose, for stars and edging. No. 2, writing, for writing, trellis work and feathering.

Large pipes
Tala ½ inch (1cm) plain for eclairs and meringues. Nos. 6, 8, 10, star pipes of varying sizes for biscuits, meringues and for decorating desserts and gateaux with cream.

No one is born with a natural skill in using icing pipes —only practice makes perfect. Do not be discouraged if your first attempt does not quite live up to professional standards—your second will be better. Practise piped decorations on an inverted cake tin, using mashed potato instead of cream or icing.

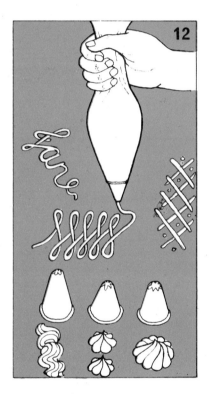

Helpful hints

Read the recipe
This is particularly important if you are making up a recipe for the first time. Read it through carefully so you understand the different stages.

Check the ingredients
Be sure you have all the ingredients necessary for the recipe before you start to cook.

Check the equipment
Be sure that you have the equipment for making the recipe.

Timing
While reading the recipe, estimate how long it will take to make and when it is likely to be ready to eat.

Butter or hard margarine
Either can be used in these recipes, though it is generally better to use butter if there is no strong flavouring in the recipe. For instance, shortbread depends on the use of butter for its flavour, whereas for gingerbread or steamed syrup pudding, margarine would do equally well.

Soft margarine
This creams readily for sponge sandwich-type cakes and can be used for shortcrust pastry and crumbles. It is also good for light fruit cakes.

Caster or granulated sugar
Use granulated sugar if it is to be melted or dissolved, for example, in fruit pies, syrups and custards. For cakes and puddings, use either granulated or caster sugar and for rich cakes, i.e. those with equal weight of fat, sugar, flour and eggs, use caster sugar.

Quantity of pastry
When a recipe calls for 4oz (100g) shortcrust or flaky pastry, this refers to the weight of flour. So, 4oz (100g) shortcrust pastry is made with 4oz (100g) plain flour, 1oz (25g) butter and 1oz (25g) lard.

To set jelly quickly
Dissolve the jelly tablet in $\frac{1}{4}$ pint ($1\frac{1}{2}$dl) hot water, then make up to 1 pint (6dl) with cold water or ice cubes. Stir until on the point of setting.

To cool custard
Pour the hot custard into a small basin. Cover the surface of the custard with cling film or foil and leave until cold. This prevents a skin forming.

Quicker creaming
Have the butter or margarine at room temperature and a thoroughly warm mixing bowl and the job is soon done.

Plate pies and flans
These are best made in a metal dish as the base pastry cooks more easily this way.

Lining cake tins
Generally this is not necessary with modern tins. Just grease them thoroughly and, if you like, put a piece of greased paper in the centre of the base of the tin. Even for Christmas cakes it is unnecessary to line the tin but, if it is a particularly large cake, tie foil or brown paper round the outside of the tin to prevent the sides of the cake becoming overbrown.

Testing to see if a cake is baked
For a rich fruit or large cake, insert a metal skewer or knitting needle in the centre. When it comes out clean the cake is done. For sponge cakes, gently touch the centre of the cake with the fingertips. When no imprint remains, the cake is done.

Traditional puddings

While we all like to serve something different, at the same time we should not lose the touch for making the sweets and puddings which time has proved to be unbeatable favourites and which have become a part of our culinary scene.

You can of course, go too far in admiring the past: mincemeat pies used to be made, as the name makes plain, with meat—hardly what we should want to eat after turkey on the 25th. The Christmas pudding itself (once plum pudding) can be made in a variety of ways and, so long as experts disagree, the rest of us can feel happily free to do a little experimenting ourselves. Lancastrians re-cook the pudding in pastry on its second day and eat it at tea; Devonians cut it into blocks, surround it with egg custard and bake it gently until set. So, even with the most traditional of our puddings, liberties can be taken.

Fruit fools, which go back to the Middle Ages, were, in more extravagant times, made with whipped cream as the main ingredient; now custard is used to make this delicious dessert. Right up to the 18th century or later, the first step in making a blanc-mange was to take a quart of cream. A typical recipe included almonds, apricot kernels and lemon peel which were all sieved and sieved again. The final touch was the addition of a glass of "mountain wine" (Malaga), a very exotic ancestor of a dish still popular today, but how costly it was in ingredients and effort.

This is true of many other traditional puddings and so they have gradually been simplified to suit our way of life. However, sometimes it can be an inspiration to look back at the earlier versions to see whether there are any good ideas worth reviving. Trifle, 200 years ago, was based on macaroons or ratafias. Its predecessor was tipsy cake, which speaks volumes about the amount of alcohol which went into it. The pancake is even older; the unleavened bread of the Bible is basically the same—just a "cake" cooked in a pan. The Irish make it with grated potato.

Names may tell you a lot about what goes into a traditional pudding. For instance, apple charlotte was originally "charlyt", an old word for custard.

Many traditional English desserts are very filling. To the French, a dessert has always been a light afterthought to a meal, but to the English it is a serious source of nourishment. This need not mean a stodgy pudding that is hard to digest; the classic Summer Pudding, though filling, is made only of bread and fruit and is so easily digested that Victorians called it "hydropathic pudding".

For those made of stouter stuff, England's winter glory is her suet puddings, from roly-polys to apple dumplings. One traditional suet pudding, now lost to us, and unlamented, was the Bedfordshire Clanger, at one end meat and onion, at the other jam. This dual-purpose pudding was once the regular dinner carried to work by hat-factory workers in Luton—one you won't find recommended as a balanced diet in this book!

Caramelised oranges (page 17), Bread and butter pudding (page 18) and Victorian trifle (page 21)

Apple charlotte

Serves 4

**4oz (100g) fresh
  breadcrumbs**
3oz (75g) brown sugar
**1¼lb (½ kilo) cooking
  apples**
2 cloves
**2oz (50g) butter or
  margarine**
**2 tablespoons golden
  syrup**
2 tablespoons water

1 Heat the oven Gas Mark 5; 375°F (190°C) and have
  ready a 1½ pint (9dl) pie dish.
2 Mix the breadcrumbs and brown sugar together.
3 Peel, core and slice the apples and arrange in layers
  with the breadcrumbs, adding the cloves and finishing
  with a generous layer of breadcrumbs. Press well into
  the dish.
4 Melt the butter or margarine, syrup and water together
  and pour over the breadcrumbs.
5 Bake towards the top of the oven for about 40 minutes.

Lemon may be used for flavouring rather than cloves,
in which case add the grated rind of ½ lemon to the
breadcrumbs and 1 tablespoon lemon juice to the syrup.

Baked apples

**1 large cooking apple per
  person**
brown sugar
butter
water

1 Heat the oven Gas Mark 5; 375°F (190°C) and have
  ready a baking dish large enough to hold the apples.
2 Wash the apples and remove the cores with a potato
  peeler or apple corer.
3 With a sharp knife slit the skin all round the apple, just
  above the middle.
4 Stand the apples in the dish. Fill the centre with brown
  sugar and top with a nut of butter.
5 Put a little water in the dish and bake for approximately
  40–45 minutes, depending on the size of the apples.
  Test with a knife to make sure the centre of the apple is
  cooked.

For a change, try baked apples with orange. Work
together 1oz (25g) butter and 1oz (25g) sugar with
the grated rind and juice of an orange and use to fill the
apples.

Eve's pudding

Serves 4

Topping:
**2oz (50g) butter or
  margarine**
2oz (50g) sugar
1 egg
**4oz (100g) self-raising
  flour**
2–3 tablespoons milk

Fruit:
1lb (½ kilo) cooking apples
3oz (75g) sugar
1–2 cloves (optional)

1 Heat the oven Gas Mark 4; 350°F (180°C) and have
  ready a greased 1½ pint (9dl) pie dish.
2 Beat the butter or margarine with the sugar until light
  and creamy. Beat in the egg.
3 Gradually stir in the flour, then add the milk, beating
  well.
4 Peel, core and slice the apples and put half in the pie
  dish. Add the sugar, then top with the remaining apples.
  Add 1–2 cloves, if liked.
5 Top with the sponge mixture, sprinkle lightly with sugar
  and bake in the centre of the oven for about 45–50 minutes.
6 Serve hot with custard.

While this pudding is traditionally made with apples, it
can also be made using just 1 apple and a can of fruit
pie filling.

Blackberry and apple pudding

Serves 6

Suet pastry:
8oz (225g) self-raising
flour
1 level teaspoon salt
4oz (100g) shredded suet
about ¼ pint (1½dl) water

Filling:
1½lb (¾ kilo) cooking
apples
6oz (175g) blackberries
6oz (175g) sugar

1 Have ready a saucepan one-third full of boiling water and a 2½ pint (1¼ litre) pudding basin.
2 Sift the flour and salt into a basin, add the suet and mix well together.
3 Add sufficient cold water to mix to a soft, pliable dough.
4 Roll out the suet pastry to a circle big enough to line the basin and cut out a quarter from 3 to 6 o'clock. Damp the cut edges of the large piece and line the basin.
5 Peel, core and slice the apples and put into the basin with the blackberries and sugar sprinkled through.
6 Roll out the remaining pastry to fit the top of the basin. Damp the edges and seal well.
7 Cover with greased greaseproof paper or foil, tie down securely and boil steadily for 2½ hours.
8 Serve hot with custard.

Try this pudding with gooseberries or plums, too.

Peach and blackcurrant compote

Serves 4–6

1lb (½ kilo) blackcurrants
5oz (150g) sugar
¼ pint (1½dl) water
6 yellow flesh peaches

1 String and tail the blackcurrants.
2 Dissolve the sugar in the water and boil steadily for 2–3 minutes.
3 Add the blackcurrants and poach very gently until tender. Leave until cold.
4 When nearly ready to serve, put the peaches into boiling water for 1 minute, then drain. The skins will come away easily. Cut the peaches in half to remove the stones, then cut into thick slices.
5 Turn the blackcurrants into a glass dish and stir in the peach slices.

Summer pudding

Serves 6

2lb (1 kilo) soft fruit
sugar
water
7–8 slices of bread

1 Prepare the fruit, then stew until tender with sugar to taste and very little water.
2 Remove and discard the crusts from the bread. Use to line a 1½ pint (9dl) pudding basin, wedging the slices together very tightly.
3 Completely fill the basin with the cooked fruit and seal the top with bread.
4 Cover with a saucer pressed down with a weight and leave in the refrigerator overnight.
5 When ready to serve, unmould the pudding on to a serving dish and serve with lightly whipped cream.

Raspberries and blackcurrants are best for this pudding. Gooseberries and strawberries can be used, or a selection of all these fruits. If the basin is rather tall, put a slice of bread in the centre of the fruit to give it stamina.

Fruit fritters

(Illustrated opposite)
Makes 12–16

Fritter batter:
4oz (100g) plain flour
1 tablespoon cooking oil
¼ pint (1½dl) warm water
2 egg whites

Fruit:
apples
bananas
oranges
pineapple

Fritter batter:
1 Mix the flour smoothly with the oil and warm water to a coating consistency.
2 Just before using, whisk the egg whites until stiff and fold them lightly into the batter.

Fruit:
Apples: peel, core and cut into rings about ¼ inch (·5cm) thick.
Bananas: peel, cut in half and split each half lengthwise.
Oranges: peel thickly to remove the pith and slice across into rings.
Pineapple: use well-drained slices of canned pineapple.

To cook the fritters:
1 Check the temperature of the deep fat which should be 340°F (175°C). To judge the heat without a thermometer, drop a teaspoonful of batter into the fat. It should rise to the surface and begin to cook and colour.
2 Coat the fruit with the fritter batter, then drain off the surplus.
3 Drop into hot fat and fry for about 5 minutes, or until golden brown, turning the fritters once during cooking.
4 Drain well and serve sprinkled with sugar.

For juicy fruits, such as oranges, it is best to dust them with flour before coating, to help the fritter batter to adhere.

Queen of puddings

Serves 3–4

¾ pint (4½dl) milk
grated rind of 1 lemon
nut of butter
2oz (50g) fresh
**   breadcrumbs**
5 level tablespoons caster
**   sugar**
2 eggs, separated
raspberry jam

1 Heat the oven Gas Mark 4; 350°F (180°C) and have ready a greased 1 pint (6dl) pie dish.
2 Heat the milk with the lemon rind and butter. Remove from the heat and add the breadcrumbs and 2 level tablespoons sugar. Leave for 30 minutes.
3 Stir in the egg yolks, then pour the mixture into the prepared dish. Bake in the centre of the oven for about 40 minutes, or until set.
4 Remove from the oven and reduce the temperature to Gas Mark 1; 275°F (140°C). Spread the top with jam.
5 Whisk the egg whites until stiff, add 2 level tablespoons sugar and continue whisking until the mixture is stiff. Lightly stir through another 1 tablespoon sugar and swirl on to the pudding. Sprinkle with sugar.
6 Return the pudding to the oven for 20 minutes, or until the meringue is crisp and lightly browned.
7 Serve while warm.

Orange rind or 1 tablespoon sherry can be used for flavouring this pudding.

Apple fritters (see recipe for Fruit fritters)

Blackberry fool

Serves 4–5

1lb (½ kilo) blackberries
4oz (100g) sugar
2 level tablespoons Bird's
**   custard powder**
¾ pint (4½dl) milk
¼ pint (1½dl) single cream

1 Cook the blackberries with the sugar over a gentle heat till the juice starts to flow, then simmer until tender. Leave to cool.
2 Mix the custard powder and 1½ level tablespoons sugar to a smooth cream with a little of the milk and put the rest on to heat.
3 When nearly boiling, pour on to the mixed custard powder, stirring well. Return the custard to the saucepan and bring to the boil, stirring all the time.
4 Cover with film and leave until cold.
5 Strain the blackberries, reserving the juice, then sieve or liquidise them.
6 Stir the fruit purée into the cold custard. Add the cream and a little blackberry juice if necessary to achieve the right consistency.
7 Turn into sundae glasses and serve chilled.

Any fruit can be used for fruit fool but strong flavoured fruits are best: redcurrants or blackcurrants, gooseberries, loganberries or damsons. Remove any stones before liquidising the fruit.

Apricot crumble

Serves 4

Fruit:
1lb (½ kilo) apricots
6 blanched almonds
3oz (75g) sugar
1–2 tablespoons water

Topping:
4oz (100g) butter or
   margarine
6oz (175g) plain flour
2oz (50g) caster sugar

1 Heat the oven Gas Mark 6; 400°F (200°C) and have ready a 1½ pint (9dl) pie dish.
2 Wash the apricots and pack evenly into the pie dish, cutting one or two if necessary. Halve the almonds and scatter with the sugar among the fruit. Add the water.
3 Rub the butter or margarine lightly into the flour until it resembles coarse breadcrumbs, then stir in the sugar.
4 Sprinkle evenly over the fruit and press down lightly.
5 Sprinkle the top with sugar and bake in the centre of the oven for 45–50 minutes.
6 Serve hot with custard.

If apricots are plentiful, use extra fruit and halve them. Remove the stones which can be cracked and the kernels then used in place of the almonds. This pudding freezes very well. Cook from frozen, adding 10–15 minutes to the cooking time.

Crispy banana pudding

Serves 4

1oz (25g) suet
4oz (100g) brown sugar
3oz (75g) fresh
   breadcrumbs
3 level tablespoons Bird's
   custard powder
4 level tablespoons sugar
1 pint (6dl) milk
2 bananas

1 Heat the oven Gas Mark 6; 400°F (200°C) and grease a 1½ pint (9dl) pie dish.
2 Chop the suet and mix with the brown sugar and breadcrumbs. Line the pie dish with the mixture, reserving some for the topping.
3 Mix the custard powder and sugar to a smooth cream with a little milk and put the rest on to heat.
4 When nearly boiling, pour on to the mixed custard powder, stirring well. Return the custard to the saucepan and bring to the boil, stirring all the time.
5 Add the sliced bananas to the custard and turn into the prepared dish.
6 Top with the remaining breadcrumb mixture and bake in the centre of the oven for 30 minutes.
7 Serve hot.

This pudding can also be made with canned fruit. Stir drained mandarins or gooseberries into the custard in place of the bananas.

Strawberry dessert

Serves 4

1¼lb (½ kilo) strawberries
2 level tablespoons sugar
1 tablespoon white wine
juice of 1 orange
juice of 1 lemon
1 tablespoon Curaçao

1 Hull the strawberries, reserving 4oz (100g) for the sauce.
2 Put the strawberries into a glass bowl and sprinkle with sugar and white wine. Turn them occasionally.
3 Make the sauce by crushing the reserved 4oz (100g) strawberries and mixing them with the orange and lemon juice and Curaçao.
4 Check the flavour and add a little sugar if necessary.
5 Serve the strawberries in dishes with the sauce poured over.

Caramelised oranges

(Illustrated on page 11)
Serves 6

8oz (225g) sugar
¼ pint (1½dl) cold water
¼ pint (1½dl) warm water
6–8 seedless oranges

1 Put the sugar in a pan with the cold water and heat gently until the sugar has dissolved. Boil steadily until it becomes a rich caramel.
2 Remove from the heat and carefully add the warm water. Return to the heat and boil until the caramel is dissolved. Leave to cool.
3 Peel the rind very thinly from 1–2 oranges and cut into very thin strips about the length of a matchstick. Add to the caramel.
4 Peel the oranges thickly, removing all the pith with the peel. Slice the oranges across thinly and arrange in a glass dish.
5 Pour the caramel over about 30 minutes before serving.

Brandy snaps (see page 71) are a very pleasant accompaniment to these oranges.

Butterscotch pudding

Serves 3–4

3½oz (90g) sugar
2 tablespoons water
2oz (50g) butter
3 level tablespoons Bird's custard powder
1 pint (6dl) milk

1 Make the butterscotch by putting 3oz (75g) sugar into a saucepan with the water and heating gently until the sugar dissolves.
2 Bring to the boil and boil steadily until it is golden brown in colour. Remove from the heat and leave until the bubbles subside. Add the butter.
3 Mix the custard powder and remaining ½oz (15g) sugar to a smooth cream with a little of the milk. Pour the rest of the milk on to the butterscotch and put on to heat.
4 When nearly boiling, pour on to the mixed custard powder, stirring well.
5 Return the mixture to the saucepan and bring to the boil, stirring all the time.
6 Pour into individual dishes and serve.

Pancakes

Makes 9

4oz (100g) plain flour
pinch of salt
1 egg
½ pint (3dl) milk
lard for frying
caster sugar
lemon juice

1 Put the flour and salt into a basin, make a well in the centre and add the egg.
2 Gradually add almost half the milk, stirring in the flour smoothly. Mix to a smooth batter.
3 Add the remaining milk and whisk for 1 minute.
4 Heat a little lard in a frying pan. When hot, pour off any excess, and pour in sufficient batter to cover the pan thinly.
5 Cook quickly until the pancake is golden brown underneath, turn or toss and cook the other side.
6 Turn on to sugared paper and sprinkle with sugar and lemon juice. Roll up and keep hot.
7 Repeat until all the pancakes are cooked.

Christmas pudding

(Illustrated on back cover)

8oz (225g) plain flour
1lb (450g) fresh
breadcrumbs
1 level teaspoon salt
4 level teaspoons mixed
spice
1 nutmeg
1 orange
1 lemon
1½lb (675g) suet
1lb (450g) brown sugar
1lb (450g) currants
8oz (225g) sultanas
1lb (450g) raisins
8oz (225g) glacé cherries
1lb (450g) prunes
4oz (100g) candied peel
2oz (50g) chopped almonds
2oz (50g) ground almonds
1½lb (675g) cooking apples
1 medium carrot
8 eggs
1 wineglass brandy
1 pint (6dl) barley wine
or milk

These ingredients will make puddings to fill basins of 7½ pints (4¼ litres) capacity. If this is too much for your family, use half quantity of all the ingredients and make two small puddings or one large one.

1 Put the flour, breadcrumbs, salt, mixed spice, grated nutmeg and the grated rind of the orange and lemon into a large bowl.
2 Chop the suet and add to the dry ingredients with the sugar. Mix thoroughly.
3 Prepare the fruit. Wash and dry the currants and sultanas, stone the raisins, cut the cherries into quarters, stone and chop the prunes, chop the candied peel and add to the dry ingredients. Mix together with the chopped and ground almonds. Stir very well.
4 Peel and core the apples, then chop them and add to the mixture, together with the grated carrot.
5 Beat the eggs and add to the pudding with the juice from the orange and lemon, the brandy and the barley wine or milk.
6 Mix thoroughly and leave for 1 day, stirring occasionally. The mixture should "squeak" when mixed—if it seems too dry, add 1–2 more eggs.
7 Turn the mixture into greased pudding basins, filling them to the brim.
8 Seal the tops of the basins well with a flour and water paste (1lb (450g) flour mixed to a stiff dough with approximately ½ pint (3dl) cold water). Cover with foil or greaseproof paper, tie down well and boil the puddings steadily for 8 hours. Remember to keep the pans topped up with boiling water.
9 Remove the coverings and the flour and water paste and leave the puddings to cool.
10 Cover with fresh foil or greaseproof paper and store in a cool, dry larder. When required, boil the puddings for 2–4 hours, depending on size.

The making of a Christmas pudding should not be hurried. It is best to have a leisurely family mixing over two or three days.

Bread and butter pudding

(Illustrated on page 11)
Serves 4

4 thin slices bread and
butter
1½oz (40g) mixed currants,
sultanas and candied
peel
2 level tablespoons sugar
2 eggs
1 pint (6dl) milk
nutmeg

1 Heat the oven Gas Mark 4; 350°F (180°C) and have ready a 1½ pint (9dl) pie dish.
2 Cut the slices of bread and butter into halves or quarters and arrange, buttered side up, in the pie dish, sprinkling the dried fruit and sugar between the layers.
3 Beat the eggs and add the milk, then pour into the pie dish. Grate a little nutmeg on top and leave to stand for 10–15 minutes.
4 Bake in the centre of the oven for 45 minutes, or until set and lightly browned.

Apple amber

Apple amber

(Illustrated above)
Serves 4–6

**5oz (150g) shortcrust
    pastry (see page 24)
1lb (½ kilo) cooking
    apples
6oz (175g) sugar
2 eggs, separated**

1 Heat the oven Gas Mark 6; 400°F (200°C) and have
   ready a deep pie plate, 7 inches (18cm) in diameter.
2 Use the pastry to line the pie plate, prick well and bake
   blind for about 25 minutes, removing the beans after
   15 minutes. Reduce the oven temperature to Gas Mark 2;
   300°F (150°C).
3 Peel, core and slice the apples and cook in as little water
   as possible until tender. Sweeten to taste with sugar.
4 Pour the hot apples on to the egg yolks, stirring well.
   Turn into the baked pastry case.
5 Whisk the egg whites until stiff, then whisk in
   2 tablespoons sugar. Stir through a further 1 tablespoon
   sugar.
6 Pile the meringue on top of the apples. Return the
   pudding to the oven and bake towards the bottom of
   the oven for 30–40 minutes, or until the meringue is
   crisp and lightly coloured.
7 Serve warm or cold.

This pudding can be made using just one egg but the
second egg makes it richer. If you are in a hurry or
slimming, omit the pastry case and make the pudding
in a pie dish.

Baked chocolate pudding

Serves 4

3oz (75g) self-raising
  flour
1 level tablespoon cocoa
2oz (50g) soft margarine
2oz (50g) sugar
1 egg
few drops vanilla essence
1 tablespoon milk

1 Heat the oven Gas Mark 4; 350°F (180°C) and have ready a greased 1½ pint (9dl) pie dish.
2 Sift the flour and cocoa into a bowl. Add the soft margarine, sugar, egg, vanilla essence and milk.
3 Using a wooden spoon, beat all the ingredients together for 1—2 minutes until a smooth, soft consistency.
4 Turn the mixture into the prepared dish and bake in the centre of the oven for about 40 minutes.
5 Serve hot with chocolate sauce.

Chocolate sauce:
Make 1 pint (6dl) Bird's custard. When it comes to the boil, add 2—3oz (50—75g) plain chocolate and stir thoroughly until the chocolate melts.

Crème brûlée

Serves 4

¾ pint (4½dl) single cream
1 bay leaf
2 eggs
4oz (100g) sugar

1 Have ready four individual soufflé dishes.
2 Flavour the cream with the bay leaf by putting both into a saucepan and heating gently, without boiling, for 15—20 minutes. Remove the bay leaf.
3 Heat the oven Gas Mark 3; 325°F (170°C).
4 Whisk the eggs and 1oz (25g) sugar together, then pour on the warm cream, whisking well.
5 Strain into the four soufflé dishes, then place them in a baking tin containing enough water to come well up the dishes.
6 Bake in the centre of the oven for about 40 minutes, or until the cream is just, but barely, set.
7 Chill until quite cold, (overnight if possible).
8 About 2 hours before serving, make the caramel topping by gently dissolving the remaining 3oz (75g) sugar in a saucepan. Continue heating, watching and shaking the saucepan until it reaches a good caramel colour. Pour a thin layer of caramel carefully on to the chilled creams. Refrigerate until required.

The traditional way to make this dessert is to sprinkle caster sugar on to the chilled cream and then to grill it until it caramelises. I find it easier to make the caramel separately.

Honeycomb mould

Serves 4—6

2 eggs, separated
2oz (50g) sugar
½oz (15g) gelatine
1 pint (6dl) milk
1 tablespoon rum

1 Have ready a 1½ pint (9dl) mould.
2 Put the egg yolks, sugar, gelatine and a little of the milk into a saucepan and mix well. Add the remaining milk and heat gently, stirring all the time.
3 Cook the custard, without letting it boil, stirring continuously, until it thickens slightly.
4 Remove from the heat and stir in the rum. Leave until it begins to set.
5 Whisk the egg whites until stiff, then fold them into the custard mixture.
6 Pour into the mould and leave until set.

Victorian trifle

(Illustrated on page 11)
Serves 6

2 level tablespoons Bird's
   custard powder
2 level tablespoons sugar
¾ pint (4½dl) milk
4 trifle sponges
3 tablespoons raspberry
   jam
4 tablespoons sherry
1 tablespoon brandy
½ pint (3dl) double cream
glacé cherries
angelica
blanched almonds

1 Mix the custard powder and sugar to a smooth cream with a little of the milk, then put the rest on to heat.
2 When nearly boiling, pour on to the mixed custard powder, stirring well. Return the custard to the saucepan and bring to the boil, stirring all the time.
3 Turn into a small basin, cover with film and leave to cool.
4 Split the trifle sponges and sandwich with jam. Arrange in a trifle bowl.
5 Soak with the sherry and brandy for about 1 hour.
6 Pour the cooled custard over and put to chill.
7 When nearly ready to serve, whisk the cream, adding a little sugar if liked, until it just holds its shape. Swirl over the custard.
8 Decorate with cherries, angelica and almonds.

Lemon soufflé

Serves 6–8

4 eggs, separated
5oz (150g) sugar
¼ pint (1½dl) water
2 lemons
½oz (15g) gelatine
½ pint (3dl) double cream
whipped cream and
   chopped nuts

1 Prepare a 6 inch (15cm) soufflé dish (see page 5).
2 Put the egg yolks, sugar, water, grated rind of the lemons and gelatine together into a large basin.
3 Set it over a saucepan of hot water and whisk until light and creamy.
4 Remove from the heat, add the juice of the lemons and continue whisking until it cools and begins to thicken.
5 Whisk the cream until it is the same consistency as the lemon mixture and lightly combine the two.
6 Whisk the egg whites until stiff and carefully fold into the lemon mixture.
7 Turn into the soufflé dish and leave to set.
8 Carefully remove the foil collar and serve decorated with whipped cream and nuts.

This soufflé freezes very well. Allow 3½–4 hours for it to defrost thoroughly.

Hot brandy soufflé

Serves 4

1oz (25g) butter
1oz (25g) plain flour
¼ pint (1½dl) milk
1oz (25g) caster sugar
3 tablespoons brandy
4 eggs, separated

1 Heat the oven Gas Mark 5; 375°F (190°C) and have ready a thoroughly greased 6 inch (15cm) soufflé dish.
2 Melt the butter in a saucepan and add the flour. Cook over a gentle heat for 1 minute, stirring constantly.
3 Gradually add the milk, beating well to keep the sauce smooth. Bring to the boil, stirring all the time.
4 Remove from the heat, then stir in the sugar and brandy. Leave until the saucepan itself is cool enough to handle comfortably.
5 Beat in the egg yolks, one at a time.
6 Whisk the egg whites until stiff and fold carefully into the soufflé mixture.
7 Turn into the prepared dish and bake in the centre of the oven for 30–40 minutes.
8 Serve immediately.

Pies, flans & tarts

In many homes, especially where there are children, the dessert is the most important part of the meal—and a pie, flan or tart is always welcome. This chapter is about pies, flans and tarts with a difference, for the variations are virtually limitless.

Most of us stick not only to the same filling but to the same pastry—shortcrust. Yet there are others: rich shortcrust pastry, sweet flan pastry and flaky pastry. Biscuit crumb crusts are increasingly used for flans and open tarts.

Shortcrust itself can vary a lot. For crisp pastry, well sifted plain and not self-raising flour should be used and the water should not be too cold. If you sweeten the pastry, the sugar must be fully dissolved otherwise it will mar the results with dark specks. Above all, when rubbing the fat into the flour to make it resemble fresh breadcrumbs, use only the fingertips and raise the mix up as you rub, to keep it cool and light. The less handling and kneading the better. Let the dough rest for half an hour, then roll it out quickly and lightly and in one direction only, with the minimum of flour on the rolling pin.

It is vital to stick to the exact amount of ingredients stated, as careless measuring results in disasters such as toughness, softness or blistering, and to mix thoroughly yet without over-handling or over-rolling. It is also important to bake the pastry for the right length of time at the right temperature, and at the position in the oven which the instruction book for your cooker recommends.

Flaky pastry is more tricky but, as there are now excellent brands of ready-made frozen flaky pastry on the market, the use of these provides an easy way out. However, if you want to try your hand at making your own, care is all that is needed to produce the most delicate, delicious pastry of all. The whole secret is to trap as much air as possible inside fine leaves of dough. To achieve this, a lot of fat is used—some in the dough itself and some dotted between the leaves of dough to keep them separate from one another and to create air pockets. Repeatedly, the dough is folded and lightly rolled and the edges sealed to trap the air inside. As with shortcrust, the pastry needs to rest after each rolling and be covered up so that a skin does not form on it. Dampen, don't grease, the baking sheet, as this pastry is greasy enough already. Keep the pastry cool all the time and handle it lightly.

Finally, here are some useful tips for making pies, flans and tarts:

1 Keep a screw-top jar of ready rubbed-in pastry in the refrigerator and just add the water to it when you use it.
2 If pressed for time, just add sugar to some of the rubbed-in pastry and use it as a crumble topping.
3 When making fruit-pies, use a pie dish with a wide rim. This will enable you to make a good looking pastry top.
4 When sweetening fruit for pies, put the sugar between the layers of fruit. If it is left on top it will make the pastry soggy.
5 A sheet of foil placed on the rack below will keep your oven clean if a fruit pie boils over during cooking.
6 To give a pie a shiny top, brush with egg or milk before cooking or sugar syrup after.

Treacle tart and Open apricot tart (page 32), and Crunchy butterscotch flan (page 29)

Shortcrust pastry

Makes 4oz (100g)

4oz (100g) flour (plain is ideal)
2oz (50g) fat (this may be all butter or margarine, or a mixture with lard)
cold water

This basic pastry is usually made with half fat to flour. All butter is perhaps best for sweet things but half butter or margarine and half lard is good too.

1 Sift the flour into a basin, then rub in the fat until it resembles fresh breadcrumbs.
2 Mix to a stiff dough with cold water. Add the water sparingly and try to wet the rubbed-in mixture equally all through before gathering it into a dough.
3 Knead lightly and use as required.

Rich shortcrust pastry

Makes 4oz (100g)

4oz (100g) flour
2½oz (65g) fat
cold water

This is usually used for fruit flans and tartlet cases. More fat is used than for ordinary shortcrust pastry but the method of making is the same.

Sweet flan pastry

Makes 4oz (100g)

4oz (100g) plain flour
3oz (75g) butter
½oz (15g) icing sugar
egg yolk and water

This is very good for rich fruit flans and tartlet cases.

1 Sift the flour into a basin and rub in the butter.
2 Sift in the icing sugar and mix lightly through.
3 Mix to a stiff dough with a little egg yolk and water.
4 Knead on a sparingly floured board and use as required.

Flaky pastry

Makes 8oz (225g)

8oz (225g) plain flour
½ level teaspoon salt
6oz (175g) hard margarine or butter
2 teaspoons lemon juice
¼ pint (1½dl) cold water

1 Sift the flour and salt into a mixing bowl, rub in a quarter of the fat and put the rest to chill.
2 Mix the pastry to a soft dough with the lemon juice and water.
3 Turn on to a lightly floured board and knead well until free from cracks. Cover and chill for 20 minutes.
4 Roll the pastry about ¼ inch (·5cm) thick to form a strip three times as long as it is wide.
5 Cut one-third of the remaining fat into small, chunky pieces and arrange evenly on two-thirds of the pastry, keeping it well in from the edge.
6 Fold the plain piece of pastry over half the fat-covered pastry and bring the rest of the fat-covered pastry down, so that it reaches the folded edge. Press the edges firmly with a rolling pin to seal in the entrapped air. Cover and chill for 20 minutes.
7 Repeat steps 4, 5 and 6 twice, starting each rolling with the pastry fold on the righthand side.
8 The pastry is now ready to use as required.

Rhubarb mandarin pie

Serves 6

10oz (275g) shortcrust
  pastry (see opposite
  page)
2lb (1 kilo) rhubarb
6oz (175g) sugar
1 can mandarin oranges

1 Heat the oven Gas Mark 6; 400°F (200°C) and have
  ready a pie plate, 8–9 inches (20–23cm) in diameter.
2 Use a third of the pastry to line the plate, taking care
  not to stretch the pastry. Press lightly on to the plate.
3 Prepare the rhubarb. Put half into the pie and sprinkle
  with sugar. Add the drained mandarin oranges and the
  rest of the rhubarb.
4 Roll out the remaining pastry to cover the top of the pie.
  Damp the edges with cold water and lay the pastry in
  position.
5 Seal the edges well, trim with a sharp knife and decorate
  the edge. Sprinkle the pie with a little water and sugar.
  Make two or three slits in the top to allow the steam to
  escape during baking.
6 Bake in the centre of the oven for 20–25 minutes, or
  until well browned, then reduce the oven temperature
  to Gas Mark 2; 300°F (150°C) and leave for about a
  further 30 minutes, or until the fruit is cooked.
7 Serve warm with custard.

The mandarin oranges seem to counteract the acidity of
the rhubarb and also make a very pretty looking pie
when cut.

Midsummer pie

(Illustrated on front cover)
Serves 6

2lb (1 kilo) mixed
  strawberries,
  raspberries and
  redcurrants
6–8oz (175–225g) sugar
8oz (225g) shortcrust
  pastry (see opposite
  page)
1 egg white
granulated sugar

1 Heat the oven Gas Mark 6; 400°F (200°C) and have
  ready a 2 pint (1 litre) pie dish.
2 Prepare the fruit, then put half of it into the pie dish.
  Sprinkle with the sugar and add the remaining fruit and
  1–2 tablespoons water.
3 Roll out the pastry to fit the top of the pie dish. Damp
  the rim of the dish with cold water, then carefully lay
  the pastry in position. Press the edge well down.
4 Trim the edge with a sharp knife, then form it into
  scallops. Brush the pie with egg white and sprinkle with
  granulated sugar. Make two slits in the top to allow the
  steam to escape during baking.
5 Bake in the centre of the oven for about 40 minutes.
6 Serve hot or cold with custard or whipped cream.

Any fruit may be used for this pie but some need more
sugar than others. Apples or gooseberries may need
longer cooking, in which case, reduce the oven temperature after 40 minutes to Gas Mark 3; 325°F (170°C)
and continue cooking for 10–15 minutes. Other fruit
combinations to try are: rhubarb with brown sugar and
cinnamon, pears and crystallised ginger, apples with
orange and orange rind, rhubarb and pears.

Chocolate cream pie

(Illustrated opposite)
Serves 6

**4oz (100g) plain
    chocolate**
2oz (50g) rice crispies
**¼ pint (1½dl) double
    cream**
**1 packet chocolate
    Angel Delight**
½ pint (3dl) milk

1 Have ready a pie plate, 8 inches (20cm) in diameter.
2 Melt the chocolate gently in a basin over hot water and stir in the rice crispies till evenly coated.
3 Turn into the pie plate, press well to the base and sides and put to chill.
4 Whisk the cream until it holds its shape and spread it evenly inside the chocolate case. Chill thoroughly.
5 When nearly ready to serve, make up the Angel Delight as directed on the packet, using the milk, and swirl into the prepared case.

Country orchard pie

Serves 4–6

**6oz (175g) shortcrust
    pastry (see page 24)**
**1–2 tablespoons
    strawberry jam**
**1lb (½ kilo) apples,
    stewed**
**2 level tablespoons Bird's
    custard powder**
2 level tablespoons sugar
¾ pint (4½dl) milk

1 Heat the oven Gas Mark 6; 400°F (200°C) and have ready a deep pie plate, 7 inches (18cm) in diameter.
2 Use the pastry to line the pie plate, prick well and bake blind for about 25 minutes, removing the beans after 15 minutes.
3 Spread the bottom of the pastry case with jam and cover with a layer of drained, stewed apple.
4 Mix the custard powder and sugar to a smooth cream with a little of the milk and put the rest on to heat.
5 When nearly boiling, pour on to the mixed custard powder, stirring well. Return the custard to the saucepan and bring to the boil, stirring all the time.
6 Pour carefully over the apples. Serve cold.

For best results, the apples should hold their shape when stewed for this pie. If they fall too quickly in the cooking, drain them before putting them in the pie.

Dutch apple pie

Serves 6–7

**10oz (275g) shortcrust
    pastry (see page 24)**
**1lb (kilo) cooking
    apples**
2oz (50g) sultanas
2oz (50g) sugar
½ level teaspoon cinnamon
**2 tablespoons golden
    syrup**
**2 level tablespoons
    demerara sugar**

1 Heat the oven Gas Mark 6; 400°F (200°C) and have ready a deep pie plate, 9 inches (23cm) in diameter.
2 Use one-third of the pastry to line the pie plate, taking care not to stretch the pastry. Press lightly into the plate.
3 Peel, core and slice the apples. Mix with the sultanas, sugar and cinnamon and put into the pastry case.
4 Roll out the remaining pastry to cover the top of the dish. Damp the edge with cold water and lay the pastry in position. Seal the edges well, trim with a sharp knife and decorate the edge.
5 Run the golden syrup on top and sprinkle with brown sugar. Make two or three slits in the top to allow the steam to escape during baking.
6 Bake in the centre of the oven for 20 minutes, then reduce the oven temperature to Gas Mark 4; 350°F (180°C) and cook for a further 20–30 minutes.
7 Serve warm with custard.

Chocolate cream pie

Strawberry angel pie

Serves 6

3 egg whites
6oz (175g) sugar
1–1¼ lb (½ kilo)
strawberries
2 tablespoons red jam
juice of ½ orange

1 Heat the oven and leave as low as possible. Draw a circle 8 inches (20cm) in diameter on a piece of grease-proof paper (a plate is a good guide). Lightly oil the paper and place on a baking sheet.
2 Whisk the egg whites until stiff, then gradually whisk in half the sugar. Continue whisking until the mixture holds its shape.
3 Lightly stir in the rest of the sugar.
4 Using the circle as a guide, spread some meringue for a base, then build up the rest into a rim, using either a teaspoon and a knife or a forcing bag and star pipe.
5 Leave in the very cool oven for 3–4 hours or longer until completely dry.
6 Just before serving, put the meringue case on to a serving dish. Hull the strawberries and arrange in the meringue case.
7 Warm the jam and orange juice together and brush over the strawberries to glaze them.

Raspberries can be used in place of strawberries. Another delicious alternative filling is poached apricots on a base of whipped cream.

Lemon meringue pie

Serves 4–6

5oz (150g) shortcrust
 pastry (see page 24)
1 packet Bird's lemon pie
 filling
1 egg, separated
½ pint (3dl) water
2 level tablespoons sugar

1 Heat the oven Gas Mark 6; 400°F (200°C) and have ready a pie plate or sandwich tin, 7 inches (18cm) in diameter.
2 Use the pastry to line the pie plate or sandwich tin, prick well and bake blind for about 25 minutes, removing the beans after 15 minutes. Reduce the oven temperature to Gas Mark 2; 300°F (150°C).
3 Put the lemon pie filling into a saucepan with the egg yolk and water.
4 Bring to the boil, stirring all the time. Turn the filling into the prepared pastry case.
5 Whisk the egg white until stiff, then gradually whisk in the sugar.
6 Top the pie with this meringue, taking care that it extends to the pastry edge.
7 Bake near the bottom of the oven for about 30 minutes, or until the meringue is crisp and lightly brown.
8 Serve warm or cold.

This is good with sultanas stirred through. For a sharper lemon pie, add the juice of ½–1 lemon to the filling before turning it into the pastry case.

Mile high strawberry pie

Serves 6

12 digestive biscuits
4oz (100g) butter
3oz (75g) caster sugar
12oz (350g) strawberries
2 egg whites
1 teaspoon lemon juice
1 sachet Dream Topping
 and 4fl.oz (110ml) milk
 or ½ pint (3dl) double
 cream

1 Heat the oven Gas Mark 5; 375°F (190°C) and have ready a pie plate, 7 inches (18cm) in diameter.
2 Crush the biscuits. Beat the butter until soft, then work in the sugar and biscuits.
3 Turn the mixture into the pie plate pressing it evenly to the base and sides. Bake in the centre of the oven for 8 minutes, then leave until cold.
4 Liquidise the strawberries and sweeten to taste.
5 Whisk the egg whites until stiff, then add the strawberries and lemon juice. Continue whisking until the mixture holds its shape.
6 Make up the Dream Topping as directed on the packet, using the milk, or whisk the cream until it begins to thicken. Stir lightly into the strawberry mixture.
7 Pile into the biscuit pie case and chill thoroughly before serving.

Apple polonaise

Serves 6

4oz (100g) shortcrust
 pastry (see page 24)
1lb (½ kilo) cooking
 apples
2oz (50g) sugar
2oz (50g) macaroons
2 tablespoons marmalade

1 Heat the oven Gas Mark 6; 400°F (200°C) and have ready a pie plate, 7–8 inches (18–20cm) in diameter.
2 Use the pastry to line the pie plate, then decorate the edge.
3 Peel, core and slice the apples and arrange in the pie case. Sprinkle with sugar.
4 Crush the macaroons, mix with marmalade and spread over the apples.
5 Bake in the centre of the oven for 30–40 minutes. Serve hot with custard.

Raspberry pear pie

Serves 6

3oz (75g) cornflakes
2oz (50g) butter
2 level tablespoons golden
  syrup
1 can pears
1 packet raspberry
  Angel Delight
½ pint (3dl) milk
cherries

1 Have ready a pie plate, 8 inches (20cm) in diameter.
2 Crush the cornflakes slightly.
3 Melt the butter and syrup gently in a saucepan, then add the cornflakes and stir until well coated.
4 Turn into the pie plate and press well to the base and sides. Chill thoroughly.
5 Drain the pears, reserving 4–5 for decoration, and cut up the remainder.
6 Make up the Angel Delight as directed on the packet, using the milk, and turn half into the chilled pie case. Add a layer of chopped pears and swirl the remaining Angel Delight on top.
7 Serve decorated with the remaining pears and a few cherries.

Cornflake crusts make a good, quick base for chilled pies.

Crunchy butterscotch flan

(Illustrated on page 23)
Serves 6–7

12 digestive biscuits
4oz (100g) butter
3oz (75g) caster sugar
1lb (½ kilo) apples, stewed
  and drained
1 packet butterscotch
  Angel Delight
½ pint (3dl) milk
8 blanched almonds,
  shredded and browned

1 Heat the oven Gas Mark 4; 350°F (180°C) and have ready a pie plate, 9 inches (23cm) in diameter.
2 Crush the biscuits. Beat the butter until soft, then work in the sugar and biscuits.
3 Turn the mixture into the pie plate, pressing evenly to the base and sides.
4 Bake for 8 minutes, then leave until cold.
5 When nearly ready to serve, spread the stewed apples in the biscuit base.
6 Make up the butterscotch Angel Delight as directed on the packet, using the milk, and swirl over the apples.
7 Scatter with browned almonds before serving.

This is also very pleasant made with stewed pears instead of apples.

Spicy Sicilian flan

Serves 6

8oz (225g) sweet flan
  pastry (see page 24)
2oz (50g) raisins
1 packet Bird's lemon pie
  filling
½ pint (3dl) water
1 sachet Dream Topping
  and 4fl.oz (110ml) milk
  or ¼ pint (1½dl) double
  cream
1 level teaspoon cinnamon

1 Heat the oven Gas Mark 6; 400°F (200°C) and have ready a flan tin, 8 inches (20cm) in diameter.
2 Use the pastry to line the flan tin, prick well and bake blind for about 30 minutes, removing the beans after 15 minutes. Leave to cool.
3 Cover the raisins with warm water and leave them to soak for 10 minutes.
4 Put the lemon pie filling into a saucepan with the water and bring to the boil, stirring all the time. Add the drained raisins.
5 Turn the lemon mixture into the baked pastry case and leave to set.
6 When ready to serve, make up the Dream Topping as directed on the packet, using the milk, or whisk the cream until it begins to thicken. Stir in the cinnamon and swirl over the pie.

Raspberry galette flan

Serves 8

**8oz (225g) sweet flan
pastry (see page 24)**
1 raspberry jelly
½ pint (3dl) hot water
**1 sachet Dream Topping
and 4fl.oz (110ml) milk
or ¼ pint (1½dl) double
cream**
¼ pint (1½dl) soured cream
1lb (½ kilo) raspberries

1 Heat the oven Gas Mark 6; 400°F (200°C) and have
ready a flan tin, 8½–9 inches (21–23cm) in diameter.
2 Use the pastry to line the flan tin, prick well and bake
blind for about 30 minutes, removing the beans after
15 minutes.
3 Dissolve the jelly in the hot water and leave to cool.
4 Make up the Dream Topping as directed on the packet,
using the milk, or whisk the cream until it begins to
thicken. Stir the soured cream into it.
5 Add two-thirds of the cool jelly and turn into the baked
pastry case. Chill until firm.
6 Cover with raspberries and glaze with the remaining
jelly.

Mandarin flan

(Illustrated on front cover)
Serves 4–5

1 can mandarin oranges
1 packet orange jelly
1 sponge flan case
apricot jam

1 Drain the mandarin oranges from the syrup.
2 Dissolve the jelly in hot water and make it up to just
under 1 pint (6dl) with the mandarin syrup and cold
water. Leave until almost set.
3 Spread the inside of the sponge flan case with apricot
jam.
4 Reserve some of the mandarin oranges for decoration
and stir the rest through the setting jelly. Turn into the
flan case.
5 When quite set, decorate with the remaining mandarin
oranges.

For a treat, make the dissolved orange jelly up to just
under 1 pint (6dl) with ginger ale and proceed as above.
Spread the sides of the flan case with jam and coat with
chopped nuts.

Blackcurrant flan

Serves 6–7

**6oz (175g) shortcrust
pastry (see page 24)**
1lb (½ kilo) blackcurrants
3oz (75g) sugar
**1 packet blackcurrant
jelly**

1 Heat the oven Gas Mark 6; 400°F (200°C) and have
ready a pie plate or sandwich tin, 8 inches (20cm) in
diameter.
2 Use the pastry to line the pie plate or sandwich tin.
Decorate the edge, prick well and bake blind for about
25 minutes, removing the beans after 15 minutes.
3 Wash and prepare the blackcurrants and stew with the
sugar and a little water until tender.
4 Strain the blackcurrants and use the juice to dissolve the
jelly. Make up to ¾ pint (4½dl) with water.
5 Stir in the blackcurrants and leave until on the point of
setting.
6 Turn into the pastry case. Serve when cold and set with
custard or cream.

Christmas slice

Christmas slice

(Illustrated above)
Serves 6

**8oz (225g) shortcrust
pastry (see page 24)**
12oz (350g) mincemeat
1 can apricots
1 egg white
granulated sugar

1 Heat the oven Gas Mark 5; 375°F (190°C) and have ready a shallow baking tin, 11 inches by 7 inches (28cm by 18cm).
2 Use three-quarters of the pastry to line the tin.
3 Mix the mincemeat with 1 tablespoon syrup from the apricots and spread into the pastry case. Arrange the drained apricots on top.
4 Roll out the remaining pastry, cut it into strips and use to make a lattice top. Damp the edges to secure them to the base.
5 Brush the lattice top with egg white and sprinkle with sugar.
6 Bake in the centre of the oven for 20 minutes, then reduce the oven temperature to Gas Mark 4; 350°F (180°C) and cook for a further 20 minutes.
7 Serve hot or cold with custard.

This can be made and frozen well in advance. Cook from frozen but add an extra 10–15 minutes to the baking time.

31

Coconut tart

Serves 6

**5oz (150g) sweet flan
   pastry (see page 24)**
1 tablespoon raspberry jam
**2oz (50g) butter or
   margarine**
2oz (50g) sugar
1 egg
**4oz (100g) desiccated
   coconut**

1 Heat the oven Gas Mark 5; 375°F (190°C) and have ready a sandwich tin, 7 inches (18cm) in diameter.
2 Use the pastry to line the sandwich tin. Spread with the jam.
3 Beat the butter or margarine and sugar together until light and creamy, then add the egg and desiccated coconut, beating well.
4 Spread the mixture over the jam and bake in the centre of the oven for 20 minutes. Reduce the oven temperature to Gas Mark 3; 325°F (170°C) and cook for a further 25–30 minutes.
5 Serve warm with custard or cold for tea.

Treacle tart

(Illustrated on page 23)
Serves 4–6

**5oz (150g) shortcrust
   pastry (see page 24)**
**3 tablespoons fresh
   breadcrumbs**
½ orange
**4 tablespoons golden
   syrup**

1 Heat the oven Gas Mark 6; 400°F (200°C) and have ready a pie plate or sandwich tin, 7 inches (18cm) in diameter.
2 Use the pastry to line the tin, pressing it well to the shape of the tin. Decorate the edge.
3 Put the breadcrumbs, juice and rind of the orange and golden syrup into the pastry case and bake in the centre of the oven for 25 minutes. Serve warm or cold.

Lemon rather than orange juice may be added to the golden syrup to counteract the sweetness.

Open apricot tart

(illustrated on page 23)
Serves 6

**6oz (175g) sweet flan
   pastry (see page 24)**
**2 level tablespoons Bird's
   custard powder**
1½ level tablespoons sugar
1 egg
¾ pint (4½dl) milk
½ tablespoon brandy
apricot jam
**1 tablespoon cream or
   top of the milk**
**15oz (425g) can apricot
   halves**
**3 level teaspoons
   arrowroot or cornflour**
1 teaspoon lemon juice
6 blanched almonds

1 Heat the oven Gas Mark 6; 400°F (200°C) and have ready a loose-bottomed flan tin, 7½ inches (19cm) in diameter.
2 Use the pastry to line the flan tin, prick well and bake blind for about 25 minutes, removing the beans after 15 minutes.
3 Mix the custard powder, sugar and egg to a smooth cream with a little of the milk and put the rest on to heat.
4 When nearly boiling, pour on to the mixed custard powder, stirring well. Return the custard to the saucepan and bring to the boil, stirring all the time.
5 Stir in the brandy, then turn into a small basin and cover with film or foil.
6 When the tart case is cold, spread the inside lightly with apricot jam.
7 Stir the cold custard briskly. Lightly stir in the cream or top of the milk and swirl into the tart case.
8 Drain the apricots and arrange them on the custard.
9 Thicken the apricot syrup with arrowroot or cornflour, stir in the lemon juice and leave to cool.
10 Shred the almonds and scatter among the apricots. Glaze with the cool syrup.

Bakewell tart

Serves 6

4oz (100g) shortcrust
  pastry (see page 24)
2 tablespoons jam
3oz (75g) butter or
  margarine
3oz (75g) sugar
1 large egg
2oz (50g) ground almonds
2oz (50g) fresh
  breadcrumbs
1 tablespoon milk
½ teaspoon almond essence
1 teaspoon lemon juice
2 teaspoons icing sugar

1 Heat the oven Gas Mark 5; 375°F (190°C) and have ready a sandwich tin or deep pie plate, 7 inches (18cm) in diameter.
2 Use the pastry to line the tin or pie plate. Prick the bottom and spread with the jam.
3 Beat the butter or margarine and sugar together until light and creamy, then beat in the egg.
4 Add the ground almonds, breadcrumbs, milk, almond essence and lemon juice, beating well.
5 Spread the mixture over the jam and bake in the centre of the oven for 40–45 minutes.
6 Sprinkle with sifted icing sugar before serving hot or cold.

Egg custard tart

Serves 4–5

5oz (150g) shortcrust
  pastry (see page 24)
¾ pint (4½dl) milk
2 eggs
1½oz (40g) sugar
nutmeg

1 Heat the oven Gas Mark 6; 400°F (200°C) and have ready a sandwich tin or deep pie plate, 7 inches (18cm) in diameter.
2 Use the pastry to line the sandwich tin or deep pie plate. Prick well and bake blind for about 25 minutes, removing the beans after 15 minutes.
3 Brush the inside of the pastry case with beaten egg. Return to the oven for 3–4 minutes. Reduce the oven temperature to Gas Mark 3; 325°F (170°C).
4 Warm the milk. Beat the eggs and sugar together, add the warm milk and pour into the pastry case.
5 Grate nutmeg on top. Return the pie to the oven and bake for about 30 minutes, or until the custard is lightly browned and set.
6 Serve hot or cold.

This quantity of egg custard fills the tart rather full before it is baked, so put in most of the custard, grate the nutmeg over and gently pour in the rest of the custard when the tart is in position in the oven.

Walnut and raisin tart

Serves 4

4oz (100g) sweet flan
  pastry (see page 24)
1oz (25g) walnuts
1oz (25g) seedless raisins
1 packet coffee
  Angel Delight
½ pint (3dl) milk
whipped cream
walnuts

1 Heat the oven Gas Mark 5; 375°F (190°C) and have ready a sandwich tin, 6 inches (15cm) in diameter.
2 Use the pastry to line the sandwich tin, prick well and bake blind for about 20 minutes, removing the beans after 10 minutes.
3 Leave the pastry case until cold.
4 Chop the walnuts coarsely and mix with the raisins.
5 Make up the Angel Delight as directed on the packet, using the milk. Stir in the nuts and raisins, then swirl into the pastry case.
6 Decorate with whipped cream and walnuts before serving.

Milk puddings, junkets & creams

Any milk-based dish makes good sense for family meals, especially if butter, eggs or cream are added. These dairy products give us many of the vitamins and much of the protein and calcium needed for body-building and growth, for strong bones and teeth, and for healthy skin, eyes, blood, nerves—and good digestion. So you can see why milk puddings are a must for growing children. Remember, too, that two eggs have as much protein as $\frac{1}{4}$lb (100g) steak and at a fraction of the price. Additionally, dairy products are especially good for elderly people. Some of the ailments of old age are caused by not eating enough of these particularly valuable foodstuffs.

Using custard powder, packet blancmanges and toppings, milk puddings are quick and easy to make, and the results are sure. Gone are the days when a Highland recipe started with the instruction: "Carry the basin to the side of the cow and milk a pint into it", or when "Crush new wheat and soak in milk and water overnight" was the first thing to do when making Frumenty, a pudding Suffolk folk used to eat during the twelve days before Christmas, leaving some outside the door for fairies.

Today, instant puddings account for over 400 million of the "pintas" that we consume each year. The use of these gives you time to add your own special touches—angelica, crumbled cornflakes, peanut brittle, sliced bananas, meringue topping, chopped nuts, strawberries or grapes. Most women now keep ready-mixes such as custard powder in their store cupboard, regarding them as just as necessary an ingredient as flour and sugar.

However, when using them remember that, easy though milk puddings are, children are more selective these days—and milk puddings can be more adult! Add lemon flavour to sago pudding, a dash of coffee to junket and an overtone of caramel to rice pudding, and you will turn them into something new and more sophisticated. Use brown sugar instead of white and you will give the pudding a toffee-like flavour.

Bread is an excellent basis for milk puddings. When bread is soaked in milk, then cooked, it takes on a light and fluffy texture, so you can even make a mock-soufflé using milk-soaked bread. As bread has valuable minerals and vitamins, as well as protein, the result is a pudding that nourishes as well as fills—even more so, if dried fruit, jam, eggs and sugar are added. Such bread-based puddings are quite different from the more familiar ones using rice, sago and other cereals, and add further variety to your repertoire.

Any dish based on milk is a thrifty one because milk in Britain is still a relatively cheap product, particularly when you consider its high food value. So, not only are the recipes in this chapter varied and interesting but they provide many of the nutriments that we need daily in our diet.

Crunchy peach custard (page 37), Cold coffee soufflé (page 36) and Velvet cream (page 41)

Cumberland pudding

Serves 4

1oz (25g) butter or
margarine
3 level tablespoons Bird's
custard powder
2 level tablespoons
self-raising flour
2oz (50g) sugar
1 pint (6dl) milk
grated rind of ½ lemon

1 Heat the oven Gas Mark 4; 350°F (180°C) and have ready a greased 1½ pint (9dl) pie dish.
2 Melt the butter or margarine gently in a saucepan, then stir in the custard powder, flour and sugar.
3 Add a little of the milk and stir until smooth. Pour on the rest of the milk and bring to the boil, stirring all the time.
4 Stir in the lemon rind and turn into the pie dish.
5 Bake for 30 minutes, or until lightly browned. Leave to settle for 10 minutes before serving.

This pudding needs to be made in a fairly large dish, as it puffs up while cooking, though it settles down again as it cools.

Cold coffee soufflé

(Illustrated on previous page)
Serves 6

2 level tablespoons Bird's
custard powder
2 eggs, separated
4 level tablespoons sugar
1 pint (6dl) milk
1 level tablespoon Bird's
instant coffee
½oz (15g) gelatine
1 sachet Dream Topping
and 4fl.oz (110ml) milk
or ½ pint (3dl) double
cream
1oz (25g) walnuts, chopped

1 Prepare a 5 inch (13cm) soufflé dish (see page 5).
2 Mix the custard powder, egg yolks and 3 level tablespoons of the sugar to a smooth cream with a little of the milk and put the rest on to heat.
3 When nearly boiling, pour on to the mixed custard powder, stirring well. Return the custard to the saucepan and bring to the boil, stirring all the time.
4 Dissolve the coffee and gelatine in a little hot water and stir into the custard. Cover with film or foil and leave to cool.
5 Whisk the egg whites until stiff, then gradually whisk in the rest of the sugar. Stir lightly into the cool custard mixture.
6 Make up the Dream Topping as directed on the packet, using the milk, or whisk the cream until it begins to thicken. Lightly stir most of it through the coffee mixture.
7 Turn into the prepared soufflé dish and leave to set.
8 To serve, remove the collar from the soufflé dish and cover the exposed sides of the soufflé with chopped walnuts. Decorate the top with the remaining Dream Topping or cream and walnuts.

Traditionally a soufflé is served in a straight sided soufflé dish. However, it can equally well be served from a glass bowl.

Baked egg custard

Serves 3–4

1 pint (6dl) milk
3 eggs
2 level tablespoons sugar
nutmeg

1 Heat the oven Gas Mark 2; 300°F (150°C) and have ready a 1 pint (6dl) pie dish.
2 Put the milk on to heat. Lightly whisk the eggs and sugar together.
3 Pour the milk on to the eggs, then strain the mixture into the pie dish.
4 Grate a little nutmeg on top and bake towards the bottom of the oven for 40 minutes.

Lemon sago meringue

Serves 4

1 pint (6dl) milk
grated rind of ½ lemon
1½oz (40g) sago
3oz (75g) sugar
1 egg, separated

1 Heat the oven Gas Mark 2; 300°F (150°C) and have ready a 1 pint (6dl) pie dish.
2 Heat the milk and lemon rind gently in a saucepan.
3 Stir the milk, then sprinkle in the sago and 1oz (25g) of the sugar. Continue stirring till the mixture comes to the boil.
4 Reduce the heat and simmer for 10 minutes, or until the grain seems clear.
5 Pour the hot pudding on to the egg yolk, stir well and turn into the pie dish.
6 Whisk the egg white until stiff, then gradually whisk in the remaining 2oz (50g) sugar. Swirl on top of the pudding and bake towards the bottom of the oven for 25–30 minutes, or until the meringue is crisp and lightly browned.

Hot pineapple pudding

Serves 4

4 level tablespoons Bird's
**   custard powder**
1 egg
2 level tablespoons sugar
¾ pint (4½dl) milk
nut of butter
13¼oz (376g) can pineapple
**   pieces**
1–2 teaspoons lemon juice

1 Mix the custard powder, egg and sugar to a smooth cream with a little of the milk and put the rest on to heat.
2 When nearly boiling, pour on to the mixed custard powder, stirring well.
3 Return the custard to the saucepan and bring to the boil, stirring all the time.
4 Add the butter and the syrup from the pineapple, then bring back to the boil.
5 Stir in the pineapple pieces and add the lemon juice to taste.
6 Turn into a serving dish and serve.

Crunchy peach custard

(Illustrated on page 35)
Serves 4

3 level tablespoons Bird's
**   custard powder**
2 level tablespoons sugar
1 pint (6dl) milk
1 can sliced peaches
demerara sugar

1 Have ready a 1½ pint (9dl) pie dish or ovenproof dish.
2 Mix the custard powder and 2 level tablespoons sugar to a smooth cream with a little of the milk and put the rest on to heat.
3 When nearly boiling, pour on to the mixed custard powder, stirring well.
4 Return the custard to the saucepan and bring to the boil, stirring all the time. Remove from the heat.
5 Drain the peaches from their syrup, cut the peach slices into halves or thirds and stir into the custard. Turn into the pie dish.
6 Leave until cold, then sprinkle liberally with demerara sugar. Grill until the sugar melts and turns golden brown.
7 Serve cool when the sugar topping is crisp.

Hawaiian pudding

Serves 4

**3 level tablespoons Bird's
  custard powder**
3 level tablespoons sugar
1 pint (6dl) milk
**2 level tablespoons
  desiccated coconut**
1 large banana
5 glacé cherries

1 Mix the custard powder and sugar to a smooth cream with a little of the milk and put the rest on to heat.
2 When nearly boiling, pour on to the mixed custard powder, stirring well. Return the custard to the saucepan and bring to the boil, stirring all the time. Cover with film and leave to cool.
3 When cold, stir well. Stir in the coconut, sliced banana and chopped cherries.
4 Serve chilled, decorated, if liked, with whipped cream, cherries and sliced banana.

Junket

(Illustrated below)
Serves 4

1 pint (6dl) milk
2 level teaspoons sugar
**1 teaspoon essence of
  rennet**
nutmeg

1 Warm the milk and sugar to blood heat. (The milk should be comfortably hot to the tip of the little finger.)
2 Pour into a glass serving dish, stir in the rennet and leave undisturbed until the junket is set.
3 Chill lightly, then grate a little nutmeg on top before serving.

For coffee junket, proceed as above but dissolve 3 teaspoons instant coffee in the milk before adding the rennet.

Junket

Hot Swiss trifle

Hot Swiss trifle

(Illustrated above)
Serves 4

½ **Swiss roll**
1 small can fruit cocktail
2 level tablespoons Bird's
   custard powder
1–2 eggs, separated
sugar
¾ **pint (4½dl) milk**

1 Heat the oven Gas Mark 3; 325°F (170°C) and have ready a 1½ pint (1 litre) pie dish.
2 Slice the Swiss roll thinly and use to line the pie dish. Cover with the drained fruit.
3 Mix the custard powder, egg yolks and 1 tablespoon sugar to a smooth cream with a very little of the milk, and put the rest on to heat.
4 When nearly boiling, pour on to the mixed custard powder, stirring well. Return the custard to the saucepan and bring to the boil, stirring all the time. Pour over the fruit.
5 Whisk the egg whites until stiff and gradually whisk in 2 level tablespoons sugar for each egg white.
6 Cover the trifle with meringue, dust with sugar and bake for about 10–15 minutes, or until lightly browned.

Two eggs give a more generous meringue but if you are using a deep rather than wide pie dish, one egg will be sufficient.

Helena's pudding

Serves 4–5

**3 level tablespoons Bird's
   custard powder
2 level tablespoons sugar
1 pint (6dl) milk
1 can blackcurrants
3 trifle sponges
whipped cream for
   decoration**

1 Mix the custard powder and sugar to a smooth cream with a little of the milk and put the rest on to heat.
2 When nearly boiling, pour on to the mixed custard powder, stirring well.
3 Return the custard to the saucepan and bring to the boil, stirring all the time. Remove from the heat, cover with film and leave until cold.
4 Drain the syrup from the blackcurrants and sprinkle it on the trifle sponges.
5 Arrange the blackcurrants, sponges and custard alternately in a serving dish.
6 Decorate with whipped cream before serving.

Creamy semolina

Serves 4

**1 pint (6dl) milk
1½oz (40g) semolina
3 level tablespoons sugar
1 small can evaporated
   milk
¼ pint (1½dl) double cream
raspberry jam**

1 Put the milk into a saucepan and bring it almost to the boil. Sprinkle in the semolina and sugar, stirring all the time.
2 Bring to the boil and cook gently for 5–6 minutes, stirring occasionally.
3 Stir in the evaporated milk. Turn the mixture into a serving dish, cover with film and allow to cool.
4 Whisk the cream until it almost holds its shape.
5 Remove the film, spread the cool semolina with jam and top with cream.

Rice pudding

Serves 4

**1¾oz (50g) short grain rice
3 level tablespoons sugar
1 pint (6dl) milk
nut of butter
nutmeg**

1 Heat the oven Gas Mark 2; 300°F (150°C) and have ready a buttered 1 pint (6dl) pie dish.
2 Put in the rice and sugar, then add the milk and nut of butter. Grate a little nutmeg on top.
3 Bake just below the centre of the oven for 2–2½ hours.

Caramelised rice:
Dissolve 2oz (50g) sugar in 1 tablespoon water in a small saucepan and boil steadily until a rich golden colour. Remove from the heat and stir in the milk. Pour the flavoured milk over the rice and add just 1oz (25g) sugar. Bake as usual.

Hazelnut creams

Serves 3

**1oz (25g) hazelnuts
1 egg white
1 level teaspoon sugar
¼ pint (1½dl) double cream
grated chocolate**

1 Warm the hazelnuts in the oven and rub off the skins. Chop coarsely and brown lightly.
2 Whisk the egg white stiffly and whisk in the sugar.
3 Whisk the cream till just beginning to thicken, then stir in the whisked egg white and the nuts.
4 Pour into three little sundae glasses and chill. Serve sprinkled generously with grated chocolate.

Crispy butterscotch whips

Serves 4

1oz (25g) butter
2oz (50g) demerara sugar
1½oz (40g) desiccated
  coconut
1½oz (40g) cornflakes
1 packet butterscotch
  Instant Whip
1 pint (6dl) milk

1 Melt the butter in a saucepan and add the sugar, coconut and cornflakes. Cook until golden brown, then leave to cool.
2 Make up the Instant Whip as directed on the packet, using the milk. Turn into serving dishes and leave to set for 5 minutes.
3 Serve sprinkled with crispy topping.

Nuts and raisins

Serves 4

1 packet chocolate
  Instant Whip
1 pint (6dl) milk
1oz (25g) peanuts
2oz (50g) seedless raisins
whipped cream

1 Make up the chocolate Instant Whip as directed on the packet, using the milk.
2 Chop the peanuts and stir into the Instant Whip, together with the raisins.
3 Serve in sundae glasses or dishes topped with whipped cream.

Velvet cream

(Illustrated on page 35)
Serves 4–6

3 level tablespoons Bird's
  custard powder
2 level tablespoons sugar
1 pint (6dl) milk
½oz (15g) gelatine
4 tablespoons sherry
1 sachet Dream Topping
  and 4fl.oz (110ml) milk
  or ½ pint (3dl) double
  cream

1 Have ready a 1¼ pint (7½dl) mould.
2 Mix the custard powder and sugar to a smooth cream, with a little of the milk and put the rest on to heat.
3 When nearly boiling, pour on to the mixed custard powder, stirring well.
4 Return the custard to the saucepan and bring to the boil, stirring all the time. Remove from the heat, cover with film and leave until cold.
5 Remove the film and stir the custard until smooth and creamy.
6 Dissolve the gelatine in the sherry in a basin over hot water.
7 Make up the Dream Topping as directed on the packet, using the milk, or whisk the cream until it begins to thicken. Fold lightly into the custard, together with the dissolved gelatine.
8 Turn the mixture into the mould and leave to set.
9 Unmould and serve decorated as liked.

Peach dessert

Serves 4

1 packet peach blancmange
  powder
3 level tablespoons sugar
1 pint (6dl) milk
5 tablespoons top of the
  milk or evaporated milk
15½oz (439g) can sliced
  peaches

1 Make up the peach blancmange as directed on the packet, using the sugar and milk. When cooked, stir in the top of the milk or evaporated milk, cover with film and leave until cold.
2 Drain the peaches from their syrup. Reserve five slices for decoration and cut the rest into pieces.
3 Stir the peach blancmange well, stir in the peach pieces and swirl into a glass bowl.
4 Serve topped with the remaining peaches.

Ice creams & chilled desserts

It is a long time since an ice cream was considered purely as a treat. Today, we, like the Americans and Italians, regard it as a serious dessert and a very popular one with children, of course. Home-made ice cream can have very high nutritional value, particularly if cream and fruit are added to it. On a hot day, cold sweets are not only a pleasure to eat but to prepare too—no working at a hot stove and no need to rush indoors early to prepare food if it is all in the refrigerator waiting.

Iced food and drink have a distinguished history. Roman Emperors used to send slaves to bring ice from the Alps, "hills candied with snow", Horace called them. Nero was very fond of snow flavoured with honey and fruit. The first ice cream eaten in England probably made its debut in Dr Johnson's time, when raspberries mixed with pure cream were frozen in a pewter basin filled with ice.

Two main types of ices are served today: the cream ice or ice cream and the water ice or sorbet. As their names imply, cream ices, being made with cream or custard, have a richer base than water ices which are basically sugar syrup flavoured with fresh fruit juices and are particularly refreshing.

The fine, creamy texture of home-made ice cream depends to a large extent on the richness of the recipe and the quickness of freezing. This is why it is wise to set the refrigerator to its coldest setting before you start to make the ice cream.

The formation of ice crystals in the sweet can be discouraged by stirring the ice cream during the freezing process. Dream Topping is a marvellous base for ice cream, as it does not form ice crystals during freezing.

Here are some hints on making ices and chilled desserts:

1 Water ices are a little more difficult to make in a domestic refrigerator but they have such a delicate, refreshing flavour that they are well worth the effort. The addition of egg white or gelatine helps to reduce the extent of crystallisation and the secret of successful water ices is frequent stirring during freezing.
2 Before starting to make ice cream, turn the refrigerator setting to freezing. Remember, though, when you serve the ice cream, to turn the setting back to normal to prevent other foods from becoming frozen.
3 Be careful not to make the ice cream too sweet, as this will inhibit freezing. Conversely, too little sugar will make an extremely hard ice cream.
4 Remember that flavours tend to be masked in frozen or very cold food, so taste the mixture before freezing to make sure it is sweet enough and very well flavoured.
5 Ice cream will expand during freezing, so do not completely fill the ice tray—leave a little room for this expansion.
6 Cover the frozen dish with foil to prevent the drying effect caused by the air circulating inside the refrigerator.
7 Jellies should be cooled before being put into the refrigerator, otherwise their steam will raise the temperature inside. They will cool more quickly if you have chilled the mould before pouring in the jelly.

Pineapple and lemon breeze (page 50), Chocolate mousse dessert (page 49), Almond and ginger creams (page 50), Peach ice cream in chocolate cups and Raspberry ice cream (page 44)

Peach ice cream in chocolate cups

(Illustrated on previous page)
Makes 7

4oz (100g) plain chocolate
¼ pint (1½dl) cream
¼ pint (1½dl) milk
1 packet peach
  Angel Delight

1 Set the refrigerator to freezing and have ready seven paper baking cases.
2 Melt the chocolate on a plate over hot water.
3 Use the melted chocolate to coat the insides of the paper cases, then turn them upside down to set, so that the edges stay thicker than the base.
4 When set, chill well, then carefully peel off the paper cases.
5 Put the cream and milk in a basin and make up the Angel Delight as directed on the packet.
6 Pipe or swirl into the prepared chocolate cups and put to freeze in the ice box.

If you own a home freezer, keep a batch of these individual ice creams in it—they make a very useful standby. They also look very pretty for a party occasion if you use different flavours of Angel Delight.

Raspberry ice cream

(Illustrated on previous page)
Serves 4

1lb (½ kilo) raspberries
4oz (100g) caster sugar
½ pint (3dl) double cream

1 Set the refrigerator to freezing and have ready a metal ice tray.
2 Liquidise most of the raspberries with the sugar or press through a sieve.
3 Stir in the cream and turn the mixture into the ice tray. Put to freeze in the ice box for 30–40 minutes.
4 When beginning to freeze at the edges, turn the mixture into a chilled bowl and whisk well.
5 Stir through the remaining whole raspberries, return the mixture to the ice tray and continue to freeze.

Custard ice cream

Serves 4–5

2 level tablespoons Bird's
  custard powder
3oz (75g) sugar
2 eggs, separated
1 pint (6dl) milk

1 Set the refrigerator to freezing and have ready a metal ice tray.
2 Mix the custard powder, 1oz (25g) of the sugar and the egg yolks to a smooth cream with a little of the milk and put the rest on to heat.
3 When nearly boiling, pour on to the mixed custard powder, stirring well.
4 Return the custard to the saucepan and bring to the boil, stirring all the time. Cover with film and leave until cold.
5 Whisk the egg whites until stiff, then whisk in the remaining sugar. Carefully fold this into the custard.
6 Turn into the ice tray and put to freeze in the ice box for 1 hour.
7 Turn the mixture into a chilled bowl and whisk thoroughly. Return to the ice tray and put to freeze.

This can be flavoured with grated orange rind or melted chocolate.

Lemon ice cream

Serves 4–5

4oz (100g) sugar
½ pint (3dl) water
3 lemons
½ pint (3dl) double cream

1 Set the refrigerator to freezing and have ready a metal ice tray.
2 Dissolve the sugar in the water and boil steadily for 10 minutes.
3 Grate the lemon rind, add it to the pan and cook for a further 2 minutes. Stir in the juice of the lemons, then remove the pan from the heat and chill.
4 When quite cold, whisk the cream and add the chilled lemon syrup, stirring well.
5 Turn into the ice tray and put to freeze in the ice box for 1–2 hours.

Coffee and ginger ice cream

Serves 3–4

3–4 pieces stem ginger
3 level teaspoons Bird's instant coffee
1 level tablespoon sugar
1 tablespoon hot water
½ pint (3dl) double cream

1 Set the refrigerator to freezing and have ready a metal ice tray.
2 Cut the ginger into pieces.
3 Dissolve the coffee and sugar in the hot water, then leave to cool.
4 Add the coffee mixture to the cream and whisk steadily till it begins to thicken.
5 Stir in the pieces of stem ginger and turn into the ice tray.
6 Put to freeze in the ice box for 1–2 hours.

If your family does not care for ginger, stir in some raisins, or, even better, raisins plumped in brandy.

Ice cream gateau

Serves 4

4 trifle sponges
raspberry jam
1 sachet Dream Topping and 4fl.oz (110ml) milk or ½ pint (3dl) double cream
1 level tablespoon sugar
1 tablespoon desiccated coconut, toasted

For this recipe you need a home freezer or a deep ice box in your refrigerator.

1 Have ready a 1lb (450g) loaf tin. Split the trifle sponges in two and spread with jam. Arrange a layer of sponge in the tin, jam side uppermost.
2 Make up the Dream Topping as directed on the packet, using the milk, or whisk the cream until thick. Stir in the sugar and spread all but 2 heaped dessertspoons over the jam.
3 Arrange another layer of sponge over the Dream Topping or cream, this time jam side down. Freeze for 15 minutes.
4 Very quickly dip the tin in hot water, then turn the cake on to a board or thick piece of foil.
5 Smooth over the sides to give the whole cake a light coating of Dream Topping or cream.
6 Spread a little of the remaining Dream Topping or cream on the top of the cake. Coat the sides with toasted coconut and decorate the top with piped stars of Dream Topping or cream.
7 Cover carefully and freeze in the normal way.
8 When required, remove from the freezer and leave at room temperature for 30 minutes before serving

Strawberry ice cream gateau

Serves 8

8 inch (20cm) sponge
  cake
2 sachets Dream Topping
8fl.oz (220ml) milk
2 level tablespoons sugar
2 cans 10oz (275g)
  strawberries
strawberry jam
chopped walnuts

For this recipe you need a home freezer or a deep ice box in your refrigerator.

1 Split the sponge cake through twice to give three layers.
2 Make up the two sachets of Dream Topping together as directed on the packet, using the milk, and whisk in the sugar.
3 Reserve a quarter of the Dream Topping and whisk the drained strawberries into the rest.
4 Spread the three layers of sponge with jam and strawberry mixture and sandwich them together, finishing with a layer of strawberry mixture.
5 Cover the sides of the gateau with strawberry mixture or jam and chopped walnuts.
6 Decorate the top of the gateau with the reserved Dream Topping.
7 Put to freeze. When required, leave at room temperature for 40 minutes before serving.

Peach ice cream sandwich

Serves 5–6

3oz (75g) plain chocolate
1½oz (40g) rice crispies
1 packet peach
  Angel Delight
½ pint (3dl) milk

1 Set the refrigerator to freezing and have ready a 1lb (450g) loaf tin lined with a strip of foil to cover the base and two sides.
2 Melt the chocolate in a basin over hot water. Add the rice crispies and stir until thoroughly coated.
3 Use half of the mixture to line the base of the prepared tin.
4 Make up the Angel Delight as directed on the packet, using the milk. Pour into the tin.
5 When set, top with the rest of the chocolate rice crispies.
6 Put to freeze in the ice box.

Raspberry ice cream pie

Serves 6–7

12 digestive biscuits
4oz (100g) butter
little cinnamon
grated nutmeg
3oz (75g) caster sugar
1 packet raspberry
  Angel Delight
½ pint (3dl) milk
3 bananas
¼ pint (1½dl) double cream

1 Set the refrigerator to freezing and have ready a pie plate, 8 inches (20cm) in diameter.
2 Crush the biscuits and work in the softened butter, the spices and sugar.
3 Press into the pie plate, then chill for 15 minutes.
4 Make up the Angel Delight as directed on the packet, using the milk. Stir in 2 sliced bananas and turn into the prepared case. Put to freeze in the ice box for about 4 hours.
5 Before serving, allow the pie to stand at room temperature for 15 minutes. Whisk the cream and spoon in swirls over the pie, then decorate with slices of the remaining banana.

Blackcurrant bombe

Blackcurrant bombe

(Illustrated above)
Serves 8

2 sachets Dream Topping
8fl.oz (220ml) milk
2 level tablespoons sugar
15oz (425g) can
   blackcurrants
2 teaspoons brandy

For this recipe you need a home freezer or a deep ice box in your refrigerator.

1 Have ready a 1½ pint (9dl) pudding bowl.
2 Make up the Dream Topping as directed on the packet, using the milk, then whisk in the sugar.
3 Use half the Dream Topping to cover the inside of the pudding bowl. Put to freeze.
4 Liquidise the blackcurrants with their syrup, then stir in the brandy.
5 Stir the blackcurrants into the remaining Dream Topping. Take the frozen Dream Topping from the freezer or ice box and turn the blackcurrant mixture into the centre.
6 Cover the bowl and freeze.
7 When ready to serve, unmould and decorate as liked.

This makes a pleasant party dessert. When frozen in a home freezer, it needs 1½ hours at room temperature to reach its ideal eating quality.

Lemon water ice

Serves 5

1 pint (6dl) water
3 lemons
6oz (175g) sugar
½oz (15g) gelatine
1 egg white

1 Set the refrigerator to freezing and have ready a metal ice tray.
2 Put the water, thinly pared lemon rind and sugar into a saucepan and heat gently until the sugar dissolves.
3 Bring to the boil and boil for 5 minutes. Strain and add the gelatine dissolved in a little water.
4 Add the juice of the lemons, then leave to cool. Turn the mixture into the ice tray and put to freeze for 30—40 minutes.
5 When beginning to freeze at the edges, turn the mixture into a chilled bowl and beat well.
6 Whisk the egg white until stiff and stir evenly through the mixture.
7 Return to the ice tray and put to freeze.

If you use medium-size lemons, which normally give 6 tablespoons lemon juice, you will have a pleasant, tangy water ice. Extra large lemons, which give 9 tablespoons juice, make a sharply flavoured ice.

Raspberry sorbet

Serves 4

1 large packet frozen raspberries, thawed
1 tablespoon lemon juice
1 egg white

1 Set the refrigerator to freezing and have ready a metal ice tray.
2 Liquidise or sieve the raspberries, stir in the lemon juice and turn the mixture into the ice tray. Put to freeze for 30—40 minutes.
3 When beginning to freeze at the edges, turn the mixture into a chilled bowl and beat well. Whisk the egg white until stiff and stir into the mixture.
4 Return to the ice tray and put to freeze.

If the raspberries have been frozen without sugar, add 3 level tablespoons caster sugar when liquidising them.

Mallow creams

Serves 4

15 marshmallows
13¼oz (376g) can pineapple pieces
12 glacé cherries
2oz (50g) blanched almonds
½ pint (3dl) double cream

1 Cut the marshmallows into quarters and put in a basin with the syrup from the pineapple.
2 Cut the pineapple pieces smaller and add to the marshmallows. Leave for 1—2 hours.
3 Cut the cherries into quarters. Chop the almonds coarsely and brown lightly.
4 Whisk the cream until it begins to hold its shape.
5 Lightly stir in the pineapple pieces, marshmallows, cherries and nuts.
6 Add enough of the pineapple syrup to give a light, creamy consistency.
7 Turn into individual glasses and chill before serving.

The easiest way to cut marshmallows is to dip the knife or scissors first into hot water.

Apricot soufflé

Serves 5

1 large can apricots
½oz (15g) gelatine
2 eggs, separated, plus
**   1 egg white**
3oz (75g) caster sugar
1 sachet Dream Topping
**   and 4fl.oz (110ml) milk**
**   or ½ pint (3dl) double**
**   cream**
brandy to taste (about
**   2 tablespoons)**
finely chopped pistachio
**   nuts or walnuts**

1 Prepare a 5 inch (13cm) soufflé dish (see page 5).
2 Drain the apricots and liquidise to a purée. This should yield ¾ pint (4½dl). If not, make up with some of the apricot syrup.
3 Dissolve the gelatine in 3 tablespoons syrup in a basin over hot water, then add to the purée.
4 Whisk the egg yolks and sugar until pale and creamy.
5 Make up the Dream Topping as directed on the packet, using the milk, or whisk the cream until it begins to thicken. Stir into the apricot purée with the brandy and whisked egg yolks.
6 Whisk the egg whites stiffly and lightly stir into the apricot mixture. Turn into the prepared soufflé dish and chill until set.
7 Remove the foil band and gently coat the exposed rim with very finely chopped pistachio nuts or walnuts.

This soufflé freezes very well and, if you wish, you can freeze it with the edges covered with nuts. It needs 5 hours at room temperature to defrost thoroughly.

Chocolate mousse dessert

(Illustrated on page 43)
Serves 4

2oz (50g) plain chocolate
4 tablespoons milk
1 egg, separated
1 level tablespoon sugar
1 trifle sponge
sponge fingers
2 tablespoons sherry
1 level teaspoon gelatine
1½ tablespoons black
**   coffee**
1 sachet Dream Topping
**   and 4fl.oz (110ml) milk**
**   or ½ pint (3dl) double**
**   cream**

1 Have ready a 1lb (450g) loaf tin lined with foil.
2 Make chocolate curls with a quarter of the chocolate and reserve them for decoration. Put the rest into a small saucepan with the milk and dissolve over a gentle heat.
3 Whisk the egg yolk and sugar until light and creamy, then stir in the chocolate milk.
4 Return the mixture to the saucepan and cook over a gentle heat without boiling, stirring all the time, until the mixture coats the back of the spoon. Leave to cool.
5 Thinly slice the trifle sponge and use to line the base of the prepared tin.
6 Cut the sponge fingers in half, dip them in sherry and use to line the sides of the tin.
7 Dissolve the gelatine in the coffee over a pan of hot water and stir into the cooled chocolate custard.
8 Make up the Dream Topping as directed on the packet, using the milk, or whisk the cream until it begins to thicken. Whisk the egg white until fluffy.
9 As the chocolate custard begins to set, gently stir in 3 large tablespoons Dream Topping or cream and the egg white. Turn the mixture into the prepared tin and chill for at least 1 hour.
10 Spread the rest of the Dream Topping or cream on top and sprinkle with chocolate curls.
11 Remove from the tin when ready to serve.

I often use thin slices of chocolate Swiss roll instead of trifle sponge to line the loaf tin. This looks pretty but a very sharp knife is needed to serve it nicely.

Pineapple and lemon breeze

(Illustrated on page 43)
Serves 4–6

1 packet lemon jelly
¼ pint (1½dl) hot water
1 small can crushed
** pineapple**
1 lemon
1 sachet Dream Topping
** and 4fl.oz (110ml) milk**
** or ¼ pint (1½dl) double**
** cream**

1 Dissolve the jelly in the hot water. Add the syrup from the pineapple and make up to 1 pint (6dl) with cold water.
2 Stir in the grated rind and juice of the lemon and leave until almost set.
3 Make up the Dream Topping as directed on the packet, using the milk, or whisk the cream until it begins to thicken. Whisk it into the setting jelly, together with the crushed pineapple.
4 Turn into a serving dish, then leave in a cool place to set.
5 Serve decorated as liked.

This dessert can be made the day before it is needed and is a refreshing party sweet.

Almond and ginger creams

(Illustrated on page 43)
Serves 4

2½ level tablespoons Bird's
** custard powder**
2 level tablespoons sugar
¾ pint (4½dl) milk
4–5 pieces stem ginger
12 blanched almonds
¼ pint (1½dl) double cream
slices of crystallised ginger

1 Mix the custard powder and sugar to a smooth cream with a little of the milk and put the rest on to heat.
2 When nearly boiling, pour on to the mixed custard powder, stirring well.
3 Return the custard to the saucepan and bring to the boil, stirring all the time.
4 Turn into a small basin, cover with film and leave until cold.
5 Cut the ginger into pieces and coarsely chop the almonds.
6 Whisk the cream until it forms soft peaks.
7 Remove the film from the custard and stir in the ginger and the almonds.
8 Lightly stir in the cream and turn into sundae glasses. Decorate each one with a slice of crystallised ginger and serve chilled.

If you can spare a tablespoon of ginger syrup, then stir this through the custard with the nuts and ginger.

Suédoise

Serves 6

1 egg white
2oz (50g) caster sugar
1oz (25g) gelatine
¼ pint (1½dl) water
1 pint (6dl) apricot
** or blackcurrant purée**
lemon juice or sugar
¼ pint (1½dl) double cream,
** whipped**

1 Heat the oven and leave as low as possible. Have ready a baking sheet lined with lightly oiled greaseproof paper or foil and a round or oblong cake tin.
2 Whisk the egg white stiffly, then add the sugar gradually, whisking all the time until the mixture is very stiff again. Using a plain tube, pipe tiny meringues on to the prepared baking sheet. Leave in the oven for about 1½–2 hours, or until completely dry.
3 Dissolve the gelatine in the water and add to the fruit purée. Taste and adjust the flavour with either lemon juice or sugar.
4 Turn the mixture into the cake tin and leave to set.
5 Unmould the suédoise on to a flat serving dish, coat with whipped cream and cover completely with the tiny meringues.

Strawberry pear crisp

Strawberry pear crisp

(Illustrated above)
Serves 6–7

12 digestive biscuits
4oz (100g) butter or
**   margarine**
3oz (75g) sugar
1 can pears
1 strawberry jelly
1 sachet Dream Topping
**   and 4fl.oz (110ml) milk**
**   or ½ pint (3dl) double**
**   cream**

1 Heat the oven Gas Mark 4; 350°F (180°C) and have ready a deep pie plate, 8 inches (20cm) in diameter.
2 Crush the biscuits and work in the softened butter or margarine and sugar. Use to line the pie plate.
3 Bake for 8 minutes, then leave until cold.
4 Drain the pears from their syrup. Dissolve the jelly in hot water and make up to 1 pint (6dl) with the syrup. Leave till almost setting.
5 Make up the Dream Topping as directed on the packet, using the milk, or whisk the cream until it begins to thicken. Use it to coat the inside of the biscuit case evenly.
6 Fill with fruit and jelly and leave to set completely.

Gossamer jelly

Serves 4

1 packet jelly
¾ pint (4½dl) hot water
2 eggs

1 Dissolve the jelly in the hot water.
2 Whisk the eggs slightly, then pour on the jelly, whisking all the time.
3 Turn into a mould or dish and chill until set.

This jelly unmoulds beautifully, without the necessity of dipping the mould in hot water.

Charlotte russe

Serves 8

1 packet lemon jelly
½ pint (3dl) hot water
cherries and angelica
2 level tablespoons Bird's
   custard powder
1 egg, separated
2 level tablespoons sugar
¾ pint (4½dl) milk
sponge fingers
2 tablespoons sherry
½ pint (3dl) double cream

1 Have ready a charlotte tin or cake tin, 6 inches (15cm) in diameter.
2 Dissolve the jelly in the hot water. Pour a very thin layer in the bottom of the tin and leave to set.
3 Arrange a decoration of cherries and angelica on the set jelly, cover carefully with a little more jelly and leave to set.
4 Mix the custard powder, egg yolk and sugar to a smooth cream with a little of the milk and put the rest on to heat.
5 When nearly boiling, pour on to the mixed custard powder, stirring well. Return the custard to the saucepan and bring to the boil, stirring all the time. Cover with film or foil and leave to cool.
6 When the decoration is set, line the sides of the tin with sponge fingers, fitting them closely together.
7 Stir the rest of the cool jelly into the cooled custard and flavour with sherry.
8 When the custard mixture is on the point of setting, whisk the cream and stir lightly through, together with the whisked egg white.
9 Turn into the prepared tin and leave until set.
10 To unmould, dip the base of the tin quickly into warm water to release the jelly, and turn on to a serving dish.
11 Tie a bow of ribbon around the sponge fingers before serving.

Honey cream peaches

Serves 4–6

15½oz (439g) can peach
   halves
juice of 2 oranges
2 level teaspoons
   desiccated coconut
¼ pint (1½dl) double cream
honey to taste

1 Open the can of peaches and drain off half the syrup. Place in a glass dish.
2 Add the orange juice and chill thoroughly.
3 Lightly brown the desiccated coconut.
4 Whisk the cream until it holds its shape and flavour delicately with honey.
5 Fill the cavities of the peaches with honey cream and sprinkle with browned coconut.

Lemons in love

Serves 5

1 packet lemon jelly
½ pint (3dl) hot water
juice of ½ lemon
1 level tablespoon Bird's
   custard powder
1 level tablespoon sugar
½ pint (3dl) milk
¼ pint (1½dl) double cream
1oz (25g) crystallised
   ginger
1oz (25g) blanched
   almonds

1 Dissolve the lemon jelly in the hot water, add the lemon juice and leave until it begins to set.
2 Mix the custard powder and sugar to a smooth cream with a little of the milk and put the rest on to heat.
3 When nearly boiling, pour on to the mixed custard powder, stirring well. Return the custard to the saucepan and bring to the boil, stirring all the time. Cover with film or foil and leave to cool.
4 Whisk the cream until it starts to thicken and stir into the cold custard.
5 Stir in the setting jelly, together with the chopped ginger and almonds.
6 Turn into sundae glasses and chill before serving.

Simple strawberry cream

Serves 4–5

8oz (225g) strawberries
1 orange
1 packet strawberry jelly
¼ pint (1½dl) hot water
1 sachet Dream Topping
  and 4fl. oz (110ml) milk
  or ¼ pint (1½dl) double
  cream

1 Liquidise the strawberries and add the juice of the orange.
2 Dissolve the jelly in the hot water, then stir in the strawberries.
3 Make up the Dream Topping as directed on the packet, using the milk, or whisk the cream until it begins to thicken. Stir gently into the jelly.
4 Turn into a glass dish and chill well before serving.

This is a pleasant way of extending a few strawberries and, piped with cream, it looks very pretty.

Pear lime cream

Serves 5–6

1 lime jelly
15oz (425g) can pears
1 sachet Dream Topping
  and 4fl.oz (110ml) milk
  or ¼ pint (1½dl) double
  cream

1 Have ready a 1½ pint (9dl) metal jelly mould.
2 Dissolve the jelly in a little hot water, then make up to ¾ pint (4½dl) with syrup from the pears and cold water. Leave until almost set.
3 Make up the Dream Topping as directed on the packet, using the milk, or whisk the cream until it begins to thicken. Whisk into the setting jelly.
4 Chop the pears and stir into the jelly cream. Turn into the mould and chill until set.

If you do not have a mould of the right size or if you prefer to serve this dessert from a glass dish, then make the mixture slightly softer by making the jelly up to 1 pint (6dl) with water and syrup from the pears.

Chilled zabaglione

Serves 3

3 egg yolks
3oz (75g) caster sugar
6–7 tablespoons Marsala

1 Whisk the egg yolks to a cream, then whisk in the sugar and Marsala.
2 Pour the mixture into a double saucepan and cook, stirring continuously, until the mixture coats the back of the spoon.
3 Pour into glasses and chill until needed.

This is a very pleasant version of the traditional whipped warm dessert. It has the advantage that it can be made well in advance.

Lemon syllabub

Serves 3

1 sachet Dream Topping
  and 4fl.oz (110ml) milk
  or ½ pint (3dl) double
  cream
1 lemon
2oz (50g) caster sugar
4 tablespoons sherry

1 Make up the Dream Topping as directed on the packet, using the milk, or whisk the cream until it begins to thicken.
2 Stir through the grated lemon rind, sugar and sherry.
3 Add the juice of the lemon (2–3 tablespoons) to taste.
4 Pour into sundae glasses and chill before serving.

Quick 'n' easy puddings

Packets of ready-to-use desserts are splendid cooking aids and there are times when, to save the day, even the most enthusiastic cook will use them as the basis for a pudding. A dessert not only helps to round off a meal but can provide the correct nutritional balance. For instance, if the main course has been scant in protein, a dessert made with milk and nuts will rectify this. After a main dish piquant in flavour, plan a bland dessert. Alternatively, if the main course is a casserole with a creamy sauce, a dessert with a crispy pastry base or a refreshing sorbet will give just the right balance.

One of the quickest desserts you can make is Instant Whip. What is not generally known, however, is that it makes a super sauce. Try Butterscotch Instant Whip poured over vanilla or coffee ice cream. You can also use it to make ice lollies for the children. Just make up a packet of Instant Whip, pour it into lolly moulds and put to freeze. Angel Delight with its creamy, light texture and full flavour, is another quick and easy dessert, invaluable as a standby.

Did you know that hot custard is a purely British institution and that it is almost unknown in the rest of the world? In this country, it belongs to puddings just as closely as butter belongs to bread, yet 125 years ago there was no such thing as custard powder. It all started because a young, ailing woman was advised by her doctor not to eat eggs. This was a great blow to her because she was very fond of egg custard. So her husband, a research chemist, applied himself to the task of finding a way of making custard without eggs. His name was Alfred Bird. When it was marketed, housewives quickly realised its versatility and began to use it as a hot, pouring sauce which is its popular use today and as British as fish and chips.

Custard powder and jelly are so well established that today they are seldom thought of as convenience foods. Most of the very early recipes for jellies are savoury but, as early as 1417, jelly appeared as a sweet dish flavoured with almonds and sugar. From then on, jelly became increasingly popular as a dessert. In the 19th century, the most elaborate copper moulds were made, many of which can be found today in antique shops.

Dream Topping is a creamy topping you can eat without watching your waistline, as it contains only a third of the calories of whipped cream. It does not need refrigeration and, when whisked with milk, it can be incorporated into any cold recipe calling for sweetened whipped cream.

The secret of providing quick puddings is to keep a well-stocked larder so that, whatever the occasion, you will be able to produce a spectacular pudding with the minimum amount of effort.

Fruit flan, Chocolate ripple and Granny's applejack (page 56)

Fruit flan

(Illustrated on previous page)
Serves 4–5

1 sponge flan case
strawberry jam
1 packet strawberry
 Angel Delight
½ pint (3dl) milk
2 bananas
glacé cherries

1 Put the flan case on a serving dish and spread the inside with jam.
2 Make up the Angel Delight as directed on the packet, using the milk.
3 Slice in 1½ bananas and swirl the mixture into the flan case.
4 Serve topped with the remaining banana and a few glacé cherries.

Chocolate ripple

(Illustrated on previous page)
Serves 3–4

¼ pint (1½dl) double cream
1 packet chocolate
 Angel Delight
½ pint (3dl) milk

1 Whisk the cream steadily until it starts to thicken.
2 Make up the Angel Delight as directed on the packet, using the milk.
3 Turn into small sundae glasses, rippling the cream through the chocolate dessert.

Granny's applejack

(Illustrated on previous page)
Serves 4

2oz (50g) butter
2oz (50g) brown sugar
3oz (75g) rolled oats
1 can apple pie filling

1 Heat the oven Gas Mark 5; 375°F (190°C) and have ready a 1½ pint (9dl) pie dish.
2 Melt the butter gently in a saucepan, then stir in the sugar and rolled oats.
3 Put the apple pie filling into the pie dish and sprinkle the oat mixture evenly over.
4 Bake for about 30–35 minutes, then serve hot with custard.

Soufflé omelette

Serves 1–2

2 eggs, separated
2 level tablespoons
 caster sugar
½oz (15g) butter
1–2 tablespoons raspberry
 jam
sifted icing sugar

1 Heat the oven Gas Mark 4; 350°F (180°C) and have ready a double thickness of kitchen paper sprinkled with caster sugar.
2 Whisk together the egg yolks and sugar until light and creamy.
3 Whisk the egg whites until stiff and lightly fold them into the egg mixture.
4 Heat the butter gently in an omelette pan, pour in the egg mixture and cook slowly over the heat for about 2 minutes. Pop the pan in the oven or under a gently heated grill for about 10 minutes, or until the omelette is risen and firm to the touch.
5 Warm the jam in a small saucepan.
6 Turn the omelette on to the sugared paper, spread with warm jam and, using the paper, gently fold the omelette in half.
7 Dust with icing sugar and serve at once.

Strawberry crunch

Serves 3–4

**1 packet strawberry
Angel Delight**
½ pint (3dl) milk
6 chocolate biscuits

1 Make up the Angel Delight as directed on the packet, using the milk.
2 Break the chocolate biscuits into pieces and stir most of them into the creamy mixture.
3 Turn into dishes. Top with the rest of the biscuits just before serving.

Honey tops

Serves 4

**1 packet strawberry
Instant Whip**
1 pint (6dl) milk
2 tablespoons clear honey
**2 tablespoons chopped
nuts**

1 Make up the Instant Whip as directed on the packet, using the milk.
2 Pour into dishes and serve topped with honey and nuts.

Crispy peaches

Serves 2

4 peach halves
1 egg white
1oz (25g) caster sugar
**1oz (25g) desiccated
coconut**

1 Heat the oven Gas Mark 3; 325°F (170°C) and have ready two ovenproof serving dishes.
2 Divide the peaches between the dishes.
3 Whisk the egg white until stiff, then add the sugar gradually, whisking all the time.
4 Carefully stir in the desiccated coconut.
5 Swirl the coconut mixture over the peaches and bake for about 20 minutes, or until lightly brown and crisp.

Tutti frutti

Serves 4

12 walnuts
10 glacé cherries
¼ pint (1½dl) double cream
**1 packet butterscotch
Angel Delight**
½ pint (3dl) milk

1 Cut the walnuts and cherries into pieces.
2 Whisk the cream until it begins to hold its shape.
3 Make up the Angel Delight as directed on the packet, using the milk, and add the walnuts, cherries and cream, stirring well.
4 Swirl into sundae glasses.

Ginger pudding with hot lemon sauce

Serves 4

1 ginger cake
**1 packet Bird's lemon pie
filling**
½ pint (3dl) water

1 Heat the oven Gas Mark 3; 325°F (170°C) and put the cake to warm for 10–15 minutes.
2 Put the lemon pie filling into a small saucepan with the water. Bring to the boil, stirring all the time.
3 Serve slices of warm gingerbread topped with the hot sauce.

If you like a very tangy lemon sauce, stir in the juice of half a lemon.

Jelly fruit whirls

(Illustrated below)
Serves 4–6

1 packet jelly
1 can fruit
1 packet Angel Delight
½ pint (3dl) milk

1 Dissolve the jelly in hot water. Make up to 1 pint (6dl) with the syrup from the fruit and cold water.
2 When the jelly is cold, stir in the fruit. Turn into sundae glasses and leave until set.
3 When nearly ready to serve, make up the Angel Delight as directed on the packet, using the milk, and pipe or swirl on to the set jelly.

Jelly jewels (illustrated on front cover):
As an alternative to the above recipe, make a stiff jelly with ¾ pint (4½dl) water. When set, chop with a sharp knife. Make up Angel Delight as directed on the packet, using ½ pint (3dl) milk. Arrange jelly in sundae glasses. Top with a layer and swirl of Angel Delight and decorate with almonds.

Jelly fruit whirls made with a variety of flavours of jelly, fruit and topping

Pineapple quickies

Pineapple quickies

(Illustrated above)
Serves 4

Swiss roll
sherry
1 small can pineapple
rings
1 sachet Dream Topping
and 4fl.oz (110ml) milk
or ¼ pint (1½dl) double
cream
toasted almonds
glacé cherries

1 Arrange four slices of Swiss roll in a serving dish and soak with sherry or syrup from the pineapple.
2 Top with the pineapple rings.
3 Make up the Dream Topping as directed on the packet, using the milk, or whisk the cream until it begins to thicken. Flavour with 1–2 teaspoons sherry and swirl on top of the pineapple.
4 Decorate each one with toasted almonds and a glacé cherry.

Highland dream

Serves 3

1 sachet Dream Topping
and 4fl.oz (110ml) milk
or ½ pint (3dl) double
cream
1–2 dessertspoons clear
honey
1–2 tablespoons whisky
12 almonds, blanched and
chopped

1 Make up the Dream Topping as directed on the packet, using the milk, or whisk the cream until it begins to thicken.
2 Stir in the honey and whisky and continue whisking until the mixture holds its shape.
3 Stir in the almonds and turn the mixture into small sundae glasses.
4 Serve or chill first, if preferred.

Taste this as you prepare it because the balance between the honey and whisky is rather delicate.

Brandied chocolate creams

Serves 3

1 packet chocolate
   Angel Delight
½ pint (3dl) milk
2 teaspoons brandy

1 Make up the Angel Delight as directed on the packet, using the milk.
2 Stir in the brandy. Serve in sundae glasses.

Ice cream sundaes

Serves 4–5

1 packet raspberry
   Instant Whip
1 pint (6dl) milk
family-size block ice cream
fresh or canned fruit
ice cream wafers

1 Make up the Instant Whip as directed on the packet, using the milk. Pour a little into each of 4–5 sundae glasses or dishes.
2 Cut the ice cream into cubes and arrange in the dishes with the fruit.
3 Top with the remaining Instant Whip and ice cream wafers.

Rialto rice

Serves 3

1 sachet Dream Topping
   and 4fl.oz (110ml) milk
   or ¼ pint (1½dl) double
   cream
15½oz (439g) can creamed
   rice
1oz (25g) sultanas
9 blanched almonds
6 glace cherries

1 Make up the Dream Topping as directed on the packet, using the milk, or whisk the cream until it begins to thicken.
2 Stir half of the Dream Topping or cream into the creamed rice, together with the sultanas, coarsely chopped almonds and cherries.
3 Turn into dishes and serve topped with the remaining Dream Topping or cream.

A simpler recipe is to stir in the grated rind of a large orange instead of the fruit and nuts.

Party mice

Serves 4

1 small can pear halves
browned almonds
currants
liquorice catherine wheel
1 packet Angel Delight
   (any flavour)
½ pint (3dl) milk

1 Drain the pears from their syrup. Decorate four of them as mice, using almonds for the ears, currants for the eyes and liquorice for the whiskers and tails.
2 Slice the remaining pears into four dishes.
3 Make up the Angel Delight as directed on the packet, using the milk. Divide between the four dishes and leave to set for 5 minutes.
4 When ready to serve, top each with a pear mouse.

Sweet'n'sour jelly

Serves 4

1 packet jelly
½ pint (3dl) hot water
1 small carton soured
   cream

1 Dissolve the jelly in the hot water and leave until beginning to set.
2 Lightly stir in the soured cream, so that the white streaks are very evident.
3 Turn into glasses and chill until set.

Poor knight's pudding

Serves 4

2 eggs
2 level teaspoons sugar
pinch of cinnamon
¼ pint (1½dl) milk
4–6 slices stale bread
fat for frying
sugar or apricot jam

1 Beat the eggs, sugar, cinnamon and milk together.
2 Remove the crusts from the bread and cut into neat fingers.
3 Soak the bread thoroughly in the egg and milk mixture, then drain. Fry in a little hot fat till golden brown on both sides.
4 Serve hot, sprinkled with sugar or sandwiched with apricot jam.

Hasty trifle

Serves 4

slices of Swiss roll
1 can fruit
1 packet raspberry
  Angel Delight
½ pint (3dl) milk

1 Arrange the slices of Swiss roll in a serving dish, cover with fruit and use a little of the syrup to soak the sponge.
2 Make up the Angel Delight as directed on the packet, using the milk, and swirl on top of the fruit.
3 Serve topped with cream, if liked.

Cherries jubilee

Serves 4

15oz (425g) can pitted
  black cherries
1oz (25g) sugar
2 level teaspoons
  cornflour
2 tablespoons brandy
vanilla ice cream

1 Drain the black cherries from their syrup.
2 Put the syrup into a small saucepan with the sugar. Stir over a low heat until the sugar dissolves, then boil steadily for 1 minute.
3 Mix the cornflour to a smooth cream with very little water. Add the syrup, stirring well.
4 Return to the saucepan and bring to the boil, stirring all the time.
5 Remove from the heat and stir in the brandy and the cherries.
6 Serve hot with vanilla ice cream.

Pineapple with kirsch

1 slice of fresh pineapple
  per person
kirsch

1 Cut the pineapple into rings about ½ inch (1cm) thick.
2 Peel the slices and remove the woody core.
3 Serve sprinkled with kirsch.

Quick lemon creams

Serves 3

1 packet Bird's lemon pie
  filling
½ pint (3dl) water
¼ pint (1½dl) double cream

1 Put the lemon pie filling and water into a saucepan and bring to the boil, stirring all the time.
2 Leave until cold. Stir well, then stir in the cream.
3 Pour into sundae glasses and serve chilled.

Fresh raspberries are an ideal topping for this lemon dessert. This mixture also makes an excellent filling for a light sponge cake.

Cakes, cookies & pastries

Our more informal ways of living today have caused many changes in our eating habits. One big difference is that, quite often, instead of a sweet or pudding, we eat cakes or biscuits along with after-dinner coffee. Furthermore, it is sometimes more convenient to invite friends in for coffee and cakes if you do not have the time to produce a formal meal. Cakes are handy as a sweet when giving a buffet party or fork supper. They are useful, too, when somebody drops in unexpectedly for a meal—if there is a cake in the tin, at least half the problem of what to give them has been solved.

Basically, there are three types of cake. First come the sponges which are made with eggs, sugar and flour, thoroughly beaten to add the fourth and very vital ingredient, air. A few sponge recipes have fat, too. Then there are creamed mixtures: these are the ones in which fat and sugar are first blended to a cream, then eggs and flour are stirred in and lastly any fruit is added. The third big group is "rubbed-in" recipes: fat and flour go in first and are rubbed together until they form crumbs, then the eggs follow to bind the mixture together. Here are some tips for cake making:

1 Grease the tin well, preferably with melted lard, then put a piece of greased paper in the base. This does not have to fit exactly.
2 Have the ingredients slightly warm before mixing them.
3 When making a fruit cake, toss the prepared fruit in a little of the measured flour. This ensures that it will be evenly distributed through the cake.
4 Use a big enough mixing bowl to allow you to mix all the ingredients together comfortably.
5 Sponge-type cakes are best eaten the day they are made.
6 Fruit cakes can be stored in a tin with a closely fitting lid for a week or two. If you wish to keep them longer, wrap them in greaseproof paper before putting in the tin.
7 Iced cakes stay fresher longer than un-iced ones.
8 When storing an iced cake, cover it with a bowl that will rest on the cake plate or board without damaging the cake or icing.

Biscuits, too, are mixed by one or other of the cake methods. If they are to be rolled and cut out, the mixture needs to be stiff. Leaving it for a while in the refrigerator will help. Biscuits need slow cooking and, to cook evenly, should all be of the same thickness. Here are some tips for biscuit making:

1 The yield of a recipe will depend on the size of the cutter used and the thickness of the biscuit. This will also, of course, affect the baking time.
2 Cut as many biscuits as possible from the first rolling of the dough.
3 Allow room for biscuits to spread on the baking sheet.
4 Remove baked biscuits from the baking sheet as soon as you take them from the oven. If the last ones stick to the tin, pop them back in the oven for a minute or two. If the biscuits are made with a creamed mixture, leave them to harden in the tin for a short while before lifting them to cool on a wire rack.
5 To keep biscuits crisp, store them in a separate tin from cakes.

Cherry and walnut cake (page 65),
Swiss roll (page 68), Macaroons (page 69) and
Nutty cherry fingers (page 70)

Victoria sandwich

4oz (100g) butter
4oz (100g) caster sugar
2 eggs
4½oz (115g) self-raising
   flour
2 tablespoons water
raspberry jam

1 Heat the oven Gas Mark 5; 375°F (190°C) and have ready two greased sandwich tins, 7 inches (18cm) in diameter.
2 Beat the butter and sugar together until light and creamy.
3 Beat in the eggs one at a time adding a little sifted flour between each addition.
4 Lightly stir in the rest of the flour, adding water to give a soft dropping consistency.
5 Divide the mixture between the sandwich tins. Bake in the centre of the oven for 18–20 minutes, or until well risen, golden brown and springy to the touch.
6 Turn on to a wire rack to cool.
7 Sandwich the two sponges together with raspberry jam and sprinkle the top lightly with caster sugar.

This is a good basic cake for freezing. For best results, freeze while still hot. Wrap when frozen.

Sand cake

6oz (175g) butter
6oz (175g) caster sugar
3 eggs
6oz (175g) cornflour
2oz (50g) plain flour
2 level teaspoons baking
   powder

1 Heat the oven Gas Mark 3; 325°F (170°C) and have ready a greased cake tin, 7 inches (18cm) in diameter.
2 Beat the butter and sugar together until light and creamy.
3 Add the eggs one at a time, beating well between each addition.
4 Lightly stir in the sifted cornflour, flour and baking powder.
5 Turn the mixture into the prepared tin. Bake just below the centre of the oven for about 1½ hours, reducing the oven temperature to Gas Mark 2; 300°F (150°C) after 1 hour.
6 Turn on to a wire rack to cool.

This cake may be flavoured with a few drops of almond or vanilla essence, or brandy.

Lemon cake

4oz (100g) butter
4oz (100g) caster sugar
1 small lemon
2 eggs
4½oz (115g) self-raising
   flour

1 Heat the oven Gas Mark 4; 350°F (180°C) and have ready a greased and lined loaf tin, 9 inches by 3½ inches (23cm by 9cm).
2 Beat the butter, sugar and grated lemon rind together until light and creamy.
3 Beat in the eggs alternately with the sifted flour.
4 Turn the mixture into the prepared tin and bake just below the centre of the oven for 35 minutes.
5 Add sufficient sugar to the juice of the lemon to make it a thick pouring consistency. Spoon this on to the cake as soon as it comes from the oven.

The lemon juice and sugar topping forms a delicious sweet and sour crust to this simple cake.

Orange seed cake

6oz (175g) butter or
  margarine
4oz (100g) sugar
1 orange
2 eggs
8oz (225g) self-raising
  flour
1 level tablespoon
  caraway seeds
2oz (50g) candied orange
  peel, chopped

1 Heat the oven Gas Mark 4; 350°F (180°C) and have ready a greased cake tin, 6 inches (15cm) in diameter.
2 Beat the butter or margarine, sugar and grated orange rind together until light and creamy.
3 Beat in the eggs, one at a time, then lightly stir in the sifted flour, adding 3 tablespoons of juice from the orange.
4 Stir in the caraway seeds and candied peel.
5 Turn the mixture into the prepared tin and bake in the centre of the oven for 50–60 minutes.
6 Turn on to a wire rack to cool.

This cake freezes well.

Sherry cake

4oz (100g) butter
4oz (100g) caster sugar
3 eggs
4oz (100g) ground almonds
8oz (225g) self-raising
  flour
4oz (100g) currants
4oz (100g) candied peel,
  chopped
4oz (100g) glacé cherries,
  chopped
$\frac{1}{4}$ pint (1$\frac{1}{2}$dl) sherry

1 Heat the oven Gas Mark 3; 325°F (170°C) and have ready a greased and lined cake tin, 8 inches (20cm) in diameter.
2 Beat the butter and sugar together until light and creamy. Beat in the eggs one at a time, adding some of the ground almonds and a little sifted flour between each addition.
3 Stir in the currants, peel and cherries together with half the sherry, then stir in the rest of the flour and ground almonds.
4 Turn the mixture into the prepared tin and bake in the centre of the oven for about 1$\frac{1}{2}$ hours.
5 Pour the rest of the sherry over the cake while it is still hot and leave in the tin till cold.

Cherry and walnut cake

(Illustrated on page 63)

8oz (225g) glacé cherries
6oz (175g) self-raising
  flour
3oz (75g) walnuts
6oz (175g) butter
6oz (175g) caster sugar
3 eggs
2oz (50g) ground almonds

1 Heat the oven Gas Mark 4; 350°F (180°C) and have ready a greased cake tin, 8 inches (20cm) in diameter.
2 Reserving 6 or 7 cherries for decoration, wash and halve the rest and toss in a little of the flour. Cut the walnuts into pieces.
3 Beat the butter and sugar together until light and creamy.
4 Beat in the eggs alternately with the sifted flour. Stir in the ground almonds, cherries and walnuts.
5 Turn the mixture into the prepared tin. Cut the reserved cherries in half and arrange on top of the mixture. Sprinkle generously with sugar.
6 Bake below the centre of the oven for 1$\frac{1}{4}$–1$\frac{1}{2}$ hours.
7 Leave to cool in the tin for 5 minutes, then turn on to a wire rack.

This cake is very pleasant made with almonds in place of walnuts, in which case decorate the top with chopped almonds and cherries before baking.

Moist coconut cake

4oz (100g) butter
4oz (100g) caster sugar
3 eggs
3oz (75g) self-raising flour
2oz (50g) ground almonds
3oz (75g) desiccated
   coconut

1 Heat the oven Gas Mark 3; 325°F (170°C) and have ready a greased cake tin, 6 inches (15cm) in diameter.
2 Beat the butter and sugar together until light and creamy.
3 Beat in the eggs alternately with the sifted flour.
4 Lightly stir in the ground almonds and desiccated coconut.
5 Turn the mixture into the prepared tin and bake in the centre of the oven for about 50 minutes.
6 Turn on to a wire rack to cool.

Gingerbread

6oz (175g) butter or
   margarine
6oz (175g) sugar
8oz (225g) black treacle
12oz (350g) plain flour
1–2 level tablespoons
   ground ginger
1 level teaspoon cinnamon
2 level teaspoons
   bicarbonate of soda
2 eggs
½ pint (3dl) milk
1 tablespoon vinegar

1 Heat the oven Gas Mark 2; 300°F (150°C) and have ready a greased 8 inch (20cm) square tin. Line two sides and the bottom of the tin with a strip of greased paper, about 6 inches (15cm) wide to ease removal of the gingerbread from the tin.
2 Put the butter or margarine, sugar and treacle into a saucepan and heat gently till the butter melts. Leave to cool.
3 Sift the flour, spices and bicarbonate of soda into a mixing bowl. Add the melted ingredients and eggs and beat well.
4 Gradually beat in the milk and vinegar, then pour the mixture into the prepared tin.
5 Bake in the centre of the oven for 1½ hours. Leave to cool in the tin for 5 minutes before turning on to a wire rack to cool.

This gingerbread develops into a rich sticky cake if wrapped in greaseproof paper and stored for 1–2 weeks before eating.

Special fruit cake

4oz (100g) glacé
   pineapple
6oz (175g) glacé cherries
4oz (100g) crystallised
   ginger
4oz (100g) mixed peel
4oz (100g) blanched
   almonds
6oz (175g) self-raising
   flour
4oz (100g) plain flour
8oz (225g) butter
5oz (150g) caster sugar
few drops almond essence
1 teaspoon lemon juice
4 eggs

1 Heat the oven Gas Mark 3; 325°F (170°C) and have ready a greased cake tin, 8 inches (20cm) in diameter.
2 Wash the sugar from the glacé pineapple, cherries, crystallised ginger and mixed peel. Cut into pieces, together with the almonds.
3 Toss the fruit in a little flour, then sift the rest.
4 Beat the butter, sugar, almond essence and lemon juice together until light and creamy.
5 Add the eggs, one at a time, beating well between each addition. Thoroughly stir in the flour and fruit.
6 Turn the mixture into the prepared tin and bake just below the centre of the oven for about 1½ hours.
7 Leave to cool in the tin for 5 minutes, then turn on to a wire rack.

This cake freezes very well and is a good standby for weekend visitors.

Dream slices

Dream slices

(Illustrated above)
Makes 16

**8oz (225g) flaky pastry
   (see page 24)**
1 egg white
caster sugar
**1 sachet Dream Topping
   and 4fl.oz (110ml) milk
   or ¼ pint (1½dl) double
   cream**
raspberry jam

1 Heat the oven Gas Mark 7; 425°F (220°C) and have
   ready two baking sheets.
2 Cut the pastry in half and roll out each piece separately,
   to an oblong 16 inches by 10 inches (40cm by 25cm).
3 Cut down the centre and then across to form 16 pieces,
   each 5 inches by 2 inches (13cm by 5cm).
4 Brush 16 pieces with water or egg white and sprinkle
   with caster sugar. Place on the baking sheets and bake
   towards the top of the oven for about 5 minutes. Leave
   to cool.
5 Make up the Dream Topping as directed on the packet,
   using the milk, or whisk the cream until it holds its shape.
6 Sandwich the pastry fingers together with raspberry jam
   and Dream Topping or cream, placing the glazed pastry
   on top.

Flapjack

Makes 16

**6oz (175g) butter or
   margarine**
6oz (175g) demerara sugar
8oz (225g) rolled oats

1 Heat the oven Gas Mark 6; 400°F (200°C) and have
   ready a greased tin, 11 inches by 7 inches (28cm by
   18cm).
2 Melt the butter or margarine and sugar together gently,
   stir in the rolled oats and press the mixture into the
   prepared tin.
3 Bake in the centre of the oven for about 30 minutes.
4 Mark into pieces while warm. Cut when cold.

Coffee and raisin cake

6oz (175g) butter or margarine
6oz (175g) sugar
3 level teaspoons Bird's instant coffee
3 eggs
8oz (225g) self-raising flour
5 tablespoons milk
4oz (100g) raisins

1 Heat the oven Gas Mark 3; 325°F (170°C) and have ready a greased cake tin, 7 inches (18cm) in diameter.
2 Beat the butter or margarine, sugar and instant coffee together until light and creamy.
3 Beat in the eggs, one at a time, adding a little sifted flour between each addition.
4 Stir in the rest of the flour, together with the milk. Lastly, stir in the raisins.
5 Bake for about $1\frac{1}{4}$ hours just below the centre of the oven.
6 Turn on to a wire rack to cool.

Molly's cake

8oz (225g) self-raising flour
$\frac{1}{2}$ level teaspoon cinnamon
2 level teaspoons mixed spice
$\frac{1}{4}$ level teaspoon nutmeg
4oz (100g) margarine
4oz (100g) brown sugar
6oz (175g) sultanas
1 egg
2 teaspoons vinegar
4 tablespoons milk
5 walnut halves

1 Heat the oven Gas Mark 4; 350°F (180°C) and have ready a greased loaf tin, $7\frac{3}{4}$ inches by 4 inches (20cm by 10cm).
2 Sift the flour and spices into a bowl, then rub in the margarine.
3 Stir in the sugar and sultanas.
4 Add the egg, vinegar and milk and beat well.
5 Turn the mixture into the prepared tin, smooth the top and arrange the walnuts down the middle.
6 Bake in the centre of the oven for 50–60 minutes.
7 Turn on to a wire rack to cool.

Swiss roll

(Illustrated on page 63)

3 eggs, separated
3oz (75g) caster sugar
3oz (75g) self-raising flour
3 tablespoons warm jam

1 Heat the oven Gas Mark 6; 400°F (200°C) and have ready a greased and lined Swiss roll tin, about 9 inches by 12 inches (23cm by 30cm).
2 Whisk the egg whites until stiff, gradually add the sugar and continue beating until the mixture is stiff.
3 Beat in the egg yolks, then very lightly fold in the sifted flour.
4 Turn the mixture into the prepared tin and bake towards the top of the oven for 12 minutes.
5 Have ready a clean, damp teatowel sprinkled with sugar. Turn the sponge on to it, short side towards you.
6 Working quickly, remove the paper, and trim the long edges with a sharp knife. Spread the surface with warm jam.
7 Almost cut through the sponge 1 inch (2cm) from the short edge. (This helps with the first turn.)
8 Roll the sponge quickly by lifting the teatowel and firmly pulling away, rather than touching the sponge.
9 Leave the Swiss roll covered with the cloth for 30 seconds, then sprinkle with caster sugar and put on a wire rack to cool.

To make a chocolate Swiss roll, use $2\frac{1}{2}$oz (65g) self-raising flour and $\frac{1}{2}$oz (15g) cocoa. Roll up without a filling. When cold, carefully unroll, spread with whipped cream and re-roll.

Shortbread

Serves 8

4oz (100g) butter
3oz (75g) caster sugar
5oz (150g) plain flour
1oz (25g) cornflour

1 Heat the oven Gas Mark 3; 325°F (170°C) and have ready a sandwich tin, 7 inches (18cm) in diameter or a baking sheet.
2 Beat the butter and sugar until light and creamy, then work in the flour and cornflour.
3 Knead the mixture lightly and either press into the sandwich tin or shape into a round flat cake about 7 inches (18cm) in diameter on the baking sheet.
4 Crimp the edge and prick well with a fork. Bake in the centre of the oven for about 1 hour in all, reducing the heat as follows:
Gas Mark 3; 325°F (170°C) for 20 minutes
Gas Mark 2; 300°F (150°C) for 20 minutes
Gas Mark 1; 275°F (140°C) for 20–25 minutes.
5 Sprinkle with caster sugar when baked and cut into wedge-shaped pieces while still warm.

Banbury cakes

Makes 8

6oz (175g) flaky pastry
  (see page 24)
2oz (50g) seedless raisins
2oz (50g) currants
1oz (25g) candied peel
2oz (50g) demerara sugar
1oz (25g) butter or
  margarine, melted
$\frac{1}{2}$ level teaspoon mixed
  spice
1 egg white
caster sugar

1 Heat the oven Gas Mark 7; 425°F (220°C) and have ready a baking sheet.
2 Combine the raisins, currants, peel, sugar, butter or margarine and spice together.
3 Roll out the pastry thinly and cut into circles, using a saucer as a guide.
4 Divide the fruit mixture between the eight rounds of pastry. Damp the edges of the pastry and draw them into the centre, sealing them well together.
5 Turn the cakes over and roll each to an oblong, shaping them to the traditional oval shape of the Banbury cake.
6 Place the cakes on the baking sheet, brush with lightly beaten egg white and sprinkle with caster sugar.
7 Make three cuts across the top of each and bake in the centre of the oven for about 15 minutes.

Eccles cakes are very similar to these, except they are round in shape and do not usually contain raisins.

Macaroons

(Illustrated on page 63)
Makes 18–20

4oz (100g) ground almonds
6oz (175g) caster sugar
2 egg whites
few drops vanilla essence
$\frac{1}{2}$ tablespoon water
blanched almonds

1 Heat the oven Gas Mark 5; 375°F (190°C) and have ready two baking sheets covered with rice paper.
2 Put the ground almonds, sugar, egg whites, vanilla essence and water into a basin and beat for approximately 5 minutes.
3 Put large teaspoonfuls of the mixture on to the prepared baking sheet. Flatten with a palette knife, brush with water and put half a blanched almond on top of each macaroon.
4 Bake in the centre of the oven for 12–15 minutes, or until lightly and evenly browned.

Nutty cherry fingers

(Illustrated on page 63)
Makes 22

6 glacé cherries
1oz (25g) nuts
4oz (100g) butter
6oz (175g) plain flour
2 level tablespoons Bird's
custard powder
3oz (75g) caster sugar

1 Heat the oven Gas Mark 3; 325°F (170°C) and have ready a shallow baking tin, approximately 11 inches by 7 inches (28cm by 18cm).
2 Cut the glacé cherries into small pieces and chop the nuts.
3 Rub the butter into the flour and custard powder.
4 Stir in the sugar, cherries and half the nuts.
5 Press the mixture into the shallow tin. Press the remaining nuts on top and bake towards the top of the oven for 25–30 minutes.
6 Sprinkle with caster sugar and leave to cool in the tin, but cut into fingers while warm.

If you do not have a Swiss-roll tin, then these fingers are better baked in a smaller rather than a larger tin.

Palmiers

Makes 8

4oz (100g) frozen puff
pastry or puff pastry
trimmings
caster sugar

1 Heat the oven Gas Mark 7; 425°F (220°C) and have ready a damp baking sheet.
2 Roll out the pastry till it is $\frac{1}{4}$ inch (·5cm) thick and about 16 inches (40cm) long. Sprinkle well with sugar, fold each end to the centre and roll lightly to seal together.
3 Again sprinkle with sugar and fold the ends to the middle. Sprinkle with sugar, dampen one side, and bring the two folded pieces together. Seal well.
4 Cut into slices $\frac{1}{4}$ inch (·5cm) thick across the folds, roll each piece lightly to flatten it, and put on the baking sheet, cut side down.
5 Sprinkle with sugar and bake for 8–10 minutes. Turn the palmiers after about 7 minutes when the underside is well browned.

These are very good to serve with rich cream desserts or ice cream.

Viennese shortcakes

Makes 9

4oz (100g) butter
2oz (50g) icing sugar
½ teaspoon vanilla essence
4oz (100g) plain flour
jam

1 Heat the oven Gas Mark 4; 350°F (180°C) and have ready bun tins lined with paper baking cases, and a forcing bag fitted with a large star pipe.
2 Beat the butter, sifted icing sugar and vanilla essence together until light and creamy.
3 Stir in the sifted flour, then put the mixture into the forcing bag and pipe in a ring in the paper cases.
4 Bake in the centre of the oven for 15–20 minutes. Leave to cool.
5 Before serving, put a little jam in the centre of each one and sprinkle with icing sugar.

This mixture can also be piped in shapes on a greased baking sheet for petits fours. Bake these for 10–12 minutes only.

Brandy snaps

Brandy snaps

(Illustrated above)
Makes 24

2oz (50g) plain flour
2oz (50g) butter or margarine
1 level teaspoon ground ginger
5oz (150g) sugar
2oz (50g) golden syrup

1 Rub the flour, butter or margarine, ginger and sugar together.
2 Add the golden syrup and bind all the ingredients together.
3 Roll into a sausage shape, wrap in foil or film and leave in the refrigerator overnight.
4 Heat the oven Gas Mark 4; 350°F (180°C) and have ready two greased baking sheets.
5 Cut the chilled mixture into 24 pieces. Roll each piece into a ball and place well apart on the baking sheets.
6 Bake for about 10 minutes, or until well spread and golden brown.
7 Allow to cool for a minute, then lift the brandy snaps off with a palette knife and quickly roll them, rough side out, round the greased handle of a wooden spoon. Slip each one off carefully and leave to cool completely.

If the brandy snaps become too cold to roll, return them to the oven for a few minutes. Fill the brandy snaps, as needed, with whipped cream flavoured with brandy, remembering that, once filled, they will soften in an hour.

Petits fours

This term covers almost any tiny fancy cake, biscuit or marzipan morsel. Here are three different types.

Almondines

Makes 25

1 egg white
2oz (50g) ground almonds
2oz (50g) caster sugar
few drops almond essence
cherries and angelica

1 Heat the oven Gas Mark 3; 325°F (170°C) and have ready a baking sheet lightly greased or covered with rice paper, and a forcing bag with a large star pipe.
2 Whisk the egg white until stiff. Stir in the almonds, sugar and almond essence.
3 Put the mixture into the forcing bag and pipe in stars, bars or rings on to the prepared baking sheet. Decorate with pieces of cherry and angelica.
4 Bake for 12–15 minutes, or until golden brown.

For a professional finish, dissolve 4 level tablespoons sugar in 2 tablespoons water and boil for $\frac{1}{2}$ minute, then brush the little biscuits with this hot syrup when you take them from the oven.

Marzipan

4oz (100g) ground almonds
2oz (50g) caster sugar
2oz (50g) icing sugar
few drops almond essence
1 teaspoon brandy
1 teaspoon lemon juice
1 egg white

1 Mix the ground almonds and caster sugar together. Stir in the sifted icing sugar.
2 Add the almond essence, brandy and lemon juice to the egg white. Whisk slightly and use to bind the ground almonds and sugar.
3 Knead until smooth.

This marzipan can be used for:

Marzipan fruits
Colour small pieces of marzipan with appropriate food colours and model miniature bananas, apples, oranges and peaches.

Stuffed dates
Carefully remove the stones from the dates and fill the cavity generously with marzipan. To finish, dip the marzipan in caster sugar.

Almond kisses
Colour the marzipan pink or pale green and sandwich blanched almonds with it. Roll the marzipan edges in caster sugar.

Caramelised grapes

12 pairs of grapes
4 tablespoons water
4oz (100g) sugar
pinch of cream of tartar

1 Check the fruit is ripe, free from blemish and dry.
2 Have ready some oiled foil or greaseproof paper and a dipping tool, such as a kitchen or pickle fork.
3 Put the water in a small saucepan, add the sugar and heat gently until completely dissolved.
4 Add the cream of tartar dissolved in a little water, then boil quickly to 290°F (148°C) and take the saucepan from the heat.
5 When the bubbles have subsided, quickly dip each piece of fruit in the syrup. Leave on the oiled paper till quite set.

Orange segments can be similarly dipped in this syrup. These fruits do not keep long in good condition, so they should be prepared on the same day as they are to be eaten.

Meringues

Makes 12–14

2 egg whites
4oz (100g) caster sugar

1 Meringues have to be dried rather than cooked, so heat the oven and leave it as low as possible.
2 Have ready a baking sheet lined with lightly oiled greaseproof paper or foil.
3 Whisk the egg whites steadily until they stand in peaks and are firm enough for the bowl to be turned upside down.
4 Add half the sugar gradually, whisking all the time. Continue whisking until the mixture is very stiff again.
5 Lightly stir in the rest of the sugar.
6 Spoon or pipe the mixture on to the prepared baking sheet and leave in the oven till completely dry, about 1½–3 hours depending on the size and the oven.

The meringues can be flavoured with coffee or chocolate before baking. Traditionally, meringues are served in pairs sandwiched with whipped cream.

Coconut meringues

Makes 14

2 egg whites
4oz (100g) caster sugar
4oz (100g) desiccated coconut
4 glacé cherries

1 Heat the oven Gas Mark 2; 300°F (150°C) and have ready a baking sheet covered with greased paper.
2 Make the meringue with the egg whites and sugar (see previous recipe) and lightly stir in the desiccated coconut.
3 Put the mixture in dessertspoonfuls on to the prepared baking sheet, drawing up the meringues to a peak or pyramid. Top each one with a piece of glacé cherry.
4 Bake for about 20 minutes towards the bottom of the oven. Lift carefully on to a wire rack to cool.

Cheesecakes

Although cheesecake is by no means absent from our traditional English puddings—indeed a cookery book published in 1893 gives recipes for twelve cheesecakes, one of which is for Lemon Cheesecake to Keep For Several Years—it is only in the last few years that cheesecakes have been rediscovered from the continent. This is partly because many delicatessens now sell cheesecake, therefore giving more people the opportunity for tasting its unusual flavour. As a result of the increasing interest in continental cookery, cheesecake is now often served with coffee either at mid-morning or in the evening.

Cheesecake originated as a Mid-European delicacy where curd cheeses and soured cream are used a great deal in cooking. Indeed, European holidays have played their part in introducing us to the wide varieties of cheesecake texture, from the solid, German-style cheesecake to the lighter adaptations.

Cheesecake also has traditional Jewish and American associations. The crisp flan case made with pastry or, in the American way, with a crushed biscuit base, contrasts pleasantly with the soft, creamy fillings. History shows that the Greek island of Samos was famous for cheesecake. At that early stage, wedding cakes were usually a form of cheesecake.

Today cheesecake makes a glamorous dessert, perfect when entertaining because it can be made well in advance and so saves any last-minute rush in the kitchen.

Here are some helpful hints for making cheesecake:

1 Cheesecakes are made from the moist, soft varieties of cheese, the unripened cheeses which are eaten fresh and should therefore be used within a few days of purchase.
2 Cream cheese is the easiest cheese to use. As its name implies it is rich in fat, so it blends well to a smooth consistency.
3 Curd cheese has more flavour than cream cheese and again blends smoothly.
4 Cottage cheese has a firm curd which is difficult to beat smooth, so it is best to sieve it. Alternatively, if you put the cottage cheese with a little cream or top of the milk in a blender or liquidiser, it will quickly become smooth.
5 When decorating the cheesecake, choose the fruit carefully because the blending of the fruit flavours with the cheese has helped to make this dessert a favourite.
6 Take care not to overchill the cheesecake. Remove it from the refrigerator about an hour before it is to be served.

Coffee cheesecake and Pineapple cheesecake (page 76), Cottage cheese pie and Tangy lemon cheesecake (page 77)

Coffee cheesecake

(Illustrated on previous page)
Serves 12

Base:
12 digestive biscuits
3oz (75g) butter

Filling:
3 eggs, separated
3oz (75g) sugar
1lb (450g) cream cheese
**1 sachet Dream Topping
    and 4fl.oz (110ml) milk
    or ½ pint (3dl) double
    cream**
½oz (15g) gelatine
2 tablespoons water
**4 level teaspoons Bird's
    instant coffee**

Decoration:
**1 can mandarin oranges
chocolate curls**

1 Heat the oven Gas Mark 4; 350°F (180°C) and have ready a loose-bottomed cake tin, 9 inches (23cm) in diameter.
2 Crush the biscuits. Beat the butter until soft, then work in the biscuits. Use to line the base of the cake tin, pressing the mixture evenly to the bottom. Bake for 8 minutes, then allow to cool.
3 Whisk the egg yolks and sugar until thick and creamy. Work in the cream cheese.
4 Make up the Dream Topping as directed on the packet, using the milk, or whisk the cream until it begins to thicken. Stir lightly into the cheese mixture.
5 Soften the gelatine in the water and dissolve over a pan of hot water. Stir thoroughly into the cheese mixture.
6 Whisk the egg whites until stiff, then fold into the mixture. Pour half the mixture over the crumb base.
7 Into the rest stir the coffee dissolved in a little water and spoon the mixture carefully on top. Place in a refrigerator to chill and set, then decorate with mandarin oranges and chocolate curls.

Half quantity of this mixture will fill a deep, 7 inch (18cm) sandwich tin.
   If you do not have a loose-bottomed cake tin, then line an ordinary tin with foil. Place one strip of foil across the tin to cover the base and two sides and another strip to cover the base and the other two sides. The cheesecake can then be easily lifted from the tin.

Pineapple cheesecake

(Illustrated on previous page)
Serves 8–10

Base:
8 digestive biscuits
2oz (50g) butter
2oz (50g) caster sugar

Filling:
1lb (450g) cottage cheese
1 lemon
**8oz (227g) can pineapple
    pieces**
½oz (15g) gelatine
2 eggs, separated
4oz (100g) caster sugar
**1 sachet Dream Topping
    and 4fl.oz (110ml) milk
    or ½ pint (3dl) double
    cream**

Decoration:
**pineapple pieces
whipped cream**

1 Have ready a loose-bottomed cake tin, 8 inches (20cm) in diameter.
2 Crush the biscuits. Beat the butter until soft, then work in the sugar and biscuits.
3 Press the mixture into the base of the tin and put to chill.
4 Sieve the cheese and stir in the grated rind and juice of the lemon. Chop the pineapple pieces and stir through.
5 Add the gelatine to the pineapple syrup and heat gently until dissolved.
6 Whisk the egg yolks and sugar together until thick and creamy and gradually beat in the gelatine syrup. Leave to cool, stirring occasionally. Stir into the cream cheese and pineapple.
7 Whisk the egg whites until stiff and stir lightly into the mixture.
8 Make up the Dream Topping as directed on the packet, using the milk, or whisk the cream until it begins to thicken. Stir into the cheese mixture. Turn into the prepared tin and leave to chill overnight.
9 Ease the cheesecake from the tin and serve decorated with pineapple and whipped cream.

This is also very good made with canned apricots instead of pineapple.

Cottage cheese pie

(Illustrated on page 75)
Serves 5

**4oz (100g) sweet flan
    pastry (see page 24)**

Filling:
4oz (100g) cottage cheese
2 eggs
1oz (25g) caster sugar
1 lemon
¼ pint (1½dl) soured cream
1 level tablespoon flour
mixed peel

1 Heat the oven Gas Mark 5; 375°F (190°C) and have ready a sandwich tin, 7 inches (18cm) in diameter.
2 Line the sandwich tin with sweet flan pastry.
3 Sieve the cottage cheese into a bowl, then add the eggs, sugar, grated rind of the lemon and 1 tablespoon lemon juice. Beat well.
4 Stir in the soured cream, the flour and a little chopped mixed peel.
5 Turn the mixture into the pastry case and bake in the centre of the oven for 35 minutes.
6 Serve warm or cold.

If you have a little more soured cream, spread it on the surface of the cheese pie and cook for a further 3–4 minutes.

Tangy lemon cheesecake

(Illustrated on page 75)
Serves 8–10

Base:
8 digestive biscuits
2oz (50g) butter
2oz (50g) sugar

Filling:
1 lemon jelly
½ pint (3dl) hot water
1lb (450g) cream cheese
**1 sachet Dream Topping
    and 4fl.oz (110ml) milk
    or ½ pint (3dl) double
    cream**
1 can cherry pie filling

1 Heat the oven Gas Mark 4; 350°F (180°C) and have ready a loose-bottomed cake tin, 8 inches (20cm) in diameter.
2 Crush the biscuits. Beat the butter until soft, then work in the sugar and biscuits.
3 Use this mixture to line the base of the cake tin, then bake for 8 minutes. Leave until cold.
4 Dissolve the jelly in the hot water and leave until on the point of setting.
5 Work the cheese until soft and stir in the jelly. Make up the Dream Topping as directed on the packet, using the milk, or whisk the cream until it begins to thicken. Whisk into the cheese mixture.
6 Turn on to the crumb base and leave until set.
7 When ready to serve, ease from the tin and serve topped with cherry pie filling.

If you prefer a sharper cheesecake, add the juice of ½–1 lemon to the mixture. This cake freezes very well.

Spicy apple cheesecake

Serves 8

Base:
**8oz (225g) flaky pastry
    (see page 24)**

Filling:
**2oz (50g) butter or
    margarine**
2oz (50g) sugar
8oz (225g) cottage cheese
**½ pint (3dl) sweetened
    apple purée**
**3 level teaspoons
    cinnamon**
**3 level tablespoons plain
    flour**
4 eggs, separated

1 Heat the oven Gas Mark 7; 425°F (220°C) and have ready a baking tin, about 9 inches by 12 inches (23cm by 30cm).
2 Use the pastry to line the tin, reserving the trimmings for decoration.
3 Beat the butter or margarine and sugar together until light and creamy. Add the cottage cheese, apple purée, cinnamon, flour and egg yolks, beating well.
4 Whisk the egg whites until stiff, then stir into the cheese mixture.
5 Spread the mixture over the pastry case. Use the pastry trimmings to decorate the top with a lattice design.
6 Bake in the centre of the oven for 25 minutes, then reduce the oven temperature to Gas Mark 5; 375°F (190°C) and bake for a further 15 minutes.
7 Serve warm or cold.

Strawberry cheesecake

Serves 8–10

Base:
3 trifle sponges

Filling:
1 lemon jelly
½ pint (3dl) hot water
1lb (450g) cream cheese
¼ pint (1½dl) double cream
strawberries

Decoration:
strawberries
jam

1 Have ready a loose-bottomed cake tin, 8 inches (20cm) in diameter.
2 Slice the trifle sponges thinly and use to line the base of the tin.
3 Dissolve the jelly in the hot water, then leave until cool.
4 Work the cheese until soft, adding the jelly gradually. Whisk the cream until it starts to hold its shape, then stir into the cheese mixture.
5 Stir in some small strawberries and turn on to the sponge base. Chill well.
6 Carefully ease the cheesecake from the tin. Top with fresh strawberries and glaze with warm jam.

Family cheesecake

Serves 6–7

Base:
2 trifle sponges

Filling:
1oz (25g) sultanas
8oz (225g) curd cheese
1 lemon
2oz (50g) caster sugar
1 level tablespoon
  cornflour
2 tablespoons milk
1 egg, separated
1oz (25g) butter, melted

1 Heat the oven Gas Mark 4; 350°F (180°C) and have ready a deep sandwich tin, 7 inches (18cm) in diameter, lined with foil.
2 Slice the trifle sponges thinly and use to line the base of the tin.
3 Put the sultanas into a small basin, cover with hot water and leave to stand for 5 minutes.
4 Put the cheese into a basin and grate the lemon rind on to it. Add the juice of the lemon, the sugar, cornflour, milk, egg yolk and melted butter and beat well together until creamy.
5 Whisk the egg white stiffly and stir lightly through the cheese mixture, together with the drained sultanas.
6 Turn the mixture on to the sponge base and bake for 25–30 minutes, or until the mixture is just firm to the touch.
7 Remove from the oven, cool, then chill overnight in the refrigerator.

Upside down cheesecake

Serves 8–10

Filling:
½ pint (3dl) milk
1 tablespoon lemon juice
4 large eggs
5oz (150g) sugar
2 level tablespoons plain
  flour
¼ level teaspoon salt
1lb (450g) cottage cheese
4oz (100g) sultanas

Base:
8oz (225g) digestive biscuits
4oz (100g) butter

1 Heat the oven Gas Mark 3; 325°F (170°C) and have ready a greased cake tin, 8 inches (20cm) in diameter.
2 Put the milk, lemon juice, eggs, sugar, flour, salt and cottage cheese into the blender goblet or liquidiser. Blend until smooth.
3 Sprinkle the sultanas round the edge of the greased tin and carefully pour the cheese mixture over.
4 Bake in the centre of the oven for about 1–1¼ hours, or until set.
5 Crush the biscuits. Beat the butter until soft, then work in the biscuits. Spread this mixture over the cheesecake immediately it comes from the oven.
6 Turn the cheesecake out, when cold, so that the sultana decorated edge becomes the top of the cheesecake.

Honey and ginger cheesecake

Serves 5–6

Base:
8oz (225g) ginger biscuits
4oz (100g) butter

Filling:
8oz (225g) cream cheese
1 small carton natural
   yogurt
2 level tablespoons honey
½ level tablespoon gelatine
2 tablespoons water

Decoration:
¼ pint (1½dl) double cream,
   whipped
crystallised ginger

1 Have ready a flan tin 8 inches (20cm) in diameter.
2 Crush the biscuits. Beat the butter until soft, then work in the biscuits. Use this mixture to line the flan case.
3 Mix the cream cheese, yogurt and honey together.
4 Soak the gelatine in the water, then dissolve it in a basin over a pan of hot water. Stir into the cream cheese mixture.
5 Pour the mixture into the flan case and put to chill.
6 Serve decorated with whipped cream and ginger.

Lemon and honey cheesecake

Serves 5–6

Base:
4oz (100g) sweet flan
   pastry (see page 24)

Filling:
8oz (225g) cream cheese
4 tablespoons milk
2oz (50g) butter
2 level tablespoons flour
1 level tablespoon honey
2 tablespoons lemon juice
1 teaspoon grated lemon
   rind
2 eggs, separated
1oz (25g) caster sugar

1 Heat the oven Gas Mark 5; 375°F (190°C) and have ready a 7 inch (18cm) square sandwich tin.
2 Use the pastry to line the sandwich tin, prick well and bake blind for 15 minutes, removing the beans after 10 minutes.
3 Reduce the oven temperature to Gas Mark 3; 325°F (170°C).
4 Work the cream cheese and milk together. Cream the butter and beat in the cheese, flour, honey, lemon juice and rind.
5 Beat in the egg yolks, one at a time.
6 Whisk the egg whites until stiff, then whisk in the sugar. Fold into the cheese mixture.
7 Turn the filling into the partly baked pastry case and bake for about 40 minutes.
8 Serve warm or cold.

Peach cheesecake

Serves 7–8

Base:
8 digestive biscuits
2oz (50g) butter
2oz (50g) sugar

Filling:
8oz (225g) cream cheese
1 packet peach
   Angel Delight
¼ pint (1½dl) yogurt
¼ pint (1½dl) milk

1 Have ready a pie plate, 8 inches (20cm) in diameter.
2 Crush the biscuits. Beat the butter until soft, then work in the sugar and biscuits.
3 Reserve a little of the crumb mixture for decoration and use the rest to line the pie plate. Chill well.
4 Work the cream cheese until soft.
5 Make up the Angel Delight as directed on the packet, using the yogurt and milk. Stir in the cream cheese.
6 Swirl into the prepared case and chill well.
7 Sprinkle with the remaining crumb mixture before serving.

Raspberry cheese tarts

Makes 16

Base:
6oz (175g) rich shortcrust
   pastry (see page 24)

Filling:
8oz (225g) cottage cheese
little cream or top of the
   milk
1 teaspoon lemon juice
caster sugar
8oz (225g) firm raspberries
3 tablespoons raspberry jam
2 tablespoons water

1. Heat the oven Gas Mark 7; 425°F (220°C) and have ready 16 patty tins.
2. Use the pastry to line the tins, prick well and bake blind for about 10 minutes. Leave to cool.
3. Sieve the cottage cheese and add a little cream or top of the milk to make it smooth. Add the lemon juice and sugar to taste.
4. Fill each tart case with cheese and decorate with raspberries.
5. Boil the raspberry jam and water together in a saucepan for 2 minutes. Leave to cool, then use to glaze the tarts.

Curd cheese tart

Serves 6

Base:
4oz (100g) sweet flan
   pastry (see page 24)

Filling:
8oz (225g) curd cheese
1 egg
3oz (75g) caster sugar
$\frac{1}{4}$ pint (1$\frac{1}{2}$dl) soured
   cream
grated rind of 1 large
   lemon
1oz (25g) Bird's custard
   powder
currants

1. Heat the oven Gas Mark 5; 375°F (190°C) and have ready a sandwich tin, 7 inches (18cm) in diameter.
2. Line the sandwich tin with sweet flan pastry.
3. Put the cheese, egg, sugar, soured cream, grated lemon rind and custard powder into a bowl and beat together well.
4. Turn the mixture into the pastry case, sprinkle a few currants on top and bake for 35 minutes. Reduce the oven temperature to Gas Mark 3; 325°F (170°C) and cook for a further 10 minutes.
5. Serve cool or when cold.

Baked cheesecake

Serves 8–10

Base:
4oz (100g) Osborne biscuits

Filling:
1lb (450g) cottage cheese
1$\frac{1}{2}$oz (40g) butter
4oz (100g) sugar
1 egg

Decoration:
canned fruit
1 tablespoon jam

1. Heat the oven Gas Mark 4; 350°F (180°C) and have ready a well buttered, loose-bottomed 7 inch (18cm) square cake tin.
2. Crush the biscuits and use half of them to coat the inside of the cake tin.
3. Sieve the cottage cheese.
4. Cream the butter and sugar together. Beat in the cheese a little at a time and then the beaten egg.
5. Turn the cheese mixture carefully into the prepared tin and sprinkle the rest of the biscuit crumbs on top.
6. Bake for 25–30 minutes. Leave in the tin until cold, preferably overnight.
7. Remove the cheesecake from the tin and place on a serving dish.
8. Drain the fruit and arrange it on top of the cake. Boil half the fruit syrup with the jam until it thickens and will form a glaze.
9. Spoon the glaze over the fruit and leave until cold.

Ann's cheesecake

Serves 6–7

Base:
6 chocolate digestive
   biscuits
1oz (25g) plain chocolate
1oz (25g) butter or
   margarine

Filling:
½oz (15g) gelatine
3 tablespoons water
1 orange
½ lemon
2oz (50g) sugar
8oz (225g) curd cheese
¼ pint (1½dl) double cream

1 Have ready a deep pie plate or loose-bottomed sand-wich tin, 7 inches (18cm) in diameter.
2 Crush the biscuits. Melt the chocolate by placing it on a plate over a pan of hot water.
3 Work the butter or margarine and melted chocolate into the biscuits. Use this mixture to line the base of the pie plate or tin.
4 Soften the gelatine in the water in a basin, then put to warm over a pan of hot water. Stir occasionally until the gelatine has dissolved.
5 Make the juice of the orange and lemon up to ½ pint (3dl) with cold water. Add the sugar and stir until dissolved, then add the gelatine.
6 Put the cheese in a basin, add the fruit syrup and mix till smooth. Leave until it begins to set.
7 Whisk the cream until it starts to hold its shape and stir lightly into the cheese mixture.
8 Pour over the crumb base and chill well.

This looks nice decorated with thin slivers of rind cut from an orange or lemon. It freezes very well.

Grape cheesecake

Serves 7

Base:
1oz (25g) butter
1 tablespoon golden syrup
2oz (50g) cornflakes,
   finely crumbled
¼ level teaspoon cinnamon

Filling:
3oz (75g) caster sugar
½oz (15g) gelatine
2 small eggs, separated
¼ pint (1½dl) milk
12oz (350g) curd cheese
1 lemon
¼ pint (1½dl) double cream

Decoration:
8oz (225g) black and white
   grapes

1 Have ready a loose-bottomed cake tin, 7 inches (18cm) in diameter.
2 Put the butter and syrup into a saucepan and heat gently until melted. Stir in the cornflake crumbs and cinnamon and press into the base of the tin. Chill.
3 Mix the sugar and gelatine together in a basin, then add the egg yolks and milk. Beat well, then cook gently over a pan of hot water until it begins to thicken, stirring all the time.
4 Remove from the heat and set aside to cool, stirring occasionally.
5 When cool, but before it sets, gradually stir in the curd cheese, the grated rind and the juice of the lemon.
6 Whisk the cream until it begins to thicken and fold lightly into the cheese mixture.
7 Whisk the egg whites, but not stiffly, and fold into the mixture.
8 Turn into the prepared tin and chill until firm.
9 Just before serving, halve the grapes and remove the pips.
10 Remove the cheesecake from the tin and arrange the grapes on top in lines of alternate colours.

Continental gateaux

What makes continental pastries and cakes so different from ours? Basically, it is the European tradition of much richer, creamier confections, less filling than ours, perhaps, but with a more festive air. Many are suitable as desserts after dinner.

The word "gateau" conjures up something that is much more than a cake, since it is usually elaborately filled and decorated. The basic cake mixture is featherlight (most often, a whisked sponge), or the base may be sweet pastry. Even the fillings and toppings have a melt-in-the-mouth quality—perhaps using buttercream inside or soft frosting on top. These are not cakes to keep but made to be eaten on the same day.

It is not only France which has built up the continental pâtisserie tradition. Each country has produced its own specialities. The light-hearted Austrians are famous for their cakes made with far less flour and far more eggs than we would think of using. In the Balkans, the accent is on a sugary sweetness that is almost overpowering. Germany has a splendid repertoire of rich, filling sweets. Italy's Mediterranean climate inspired her to invent ice creams and sorbets of every colour and flavour and with every kind of garnish and topping. Danish pastries are so world-famous that now everyone makes them—sweet, yeasty breads rich with icing, nuts and fruit. The Spanish like creams and fruity sweetmeats. The Swiss, with their mixed German-Italian-French heritage, get the best of all worlds.

Holidays abroad provide excellent opportunities to acquire new tastes, but it is not so easy to guess how such appetising results are achieved. So, this chapter will undoubtedly appeal to those who would like to reproduce at home some of the pleasures of bygone holidays. These continental gateaux are ideal for party occasions and, by making them some hours beforehand, the hostess does not have to desert her guests for "dishing up" operations in the kitchen.

The sponges can be based on our own familiar Victoria sponge mixture, or on a richer Genoese sponge which contains fat. Often, on the Continent, ground almonds or hazelnuts are used in place of some of the flour. Many continental sweets employ choux pastry—incredibly light, crisp bubbles of air. An idea which we can well copy is the continental habit of using a round of rich shortcrust pastry or flan pastry as a base for a gateau. Sandwich a light sponge cake to the crisp base with lemon curd or a smooth jam and decorate appropriately. This simplifies the serving of rich gateau. I know you will enjoy all these recipes—just as long as you turn a blind eye to the calories!

Strawberry meringue gateau and Chestnut gateau (page 85), Frangipan tartlets (page 86) and Orange gateau (page 84)

Orange gateau

(Illustrated on previous page)

Cake:
4oz (100g) butter or
margarine
4oz (100g) caster sugar
1 orange
3 eggs
6oz (175g) self-raising
flour

Filling:
3oz (75g) butter
4oz (100g) icing sugar
1 egg yolk
1 tablespoon top of the
milk
2 teaspoons orange juice

Icing:
12oz (350g) icing sugar
1 egg white
orange juice
orange colouring

Decoration:
apricot jam
desiccated coconut,
coloured green
crystallised orange slices
angelica

Cake:
1 Heat the oven Gas Mark 4; 350°F (180°C) and have ready a greased 7 inch (18cm) square cake tin.
2 Beat the butter or margarine, sugar and grated orange rind together until light and creamy.
3 Beat in the eggs, one at a time, adding a little sifted flour between each addition.
4 Lightly stir in the remaining flour with 2 tablespoons of the juice from the orange.
5 Turn the mixture into the prepared tin and bake in the centre of the oven for 40 minutes, or until golden brown and springy to the touch.
6 Turn on to a wire rack to cool.

Filling:
1 Beat the butter and sifted icing sugar together until light and creamy.
2 Beat in the egg yolk, the top of the milk and lastly the orange juice.

Icing:
1 Sift the icing sugar and mix smoothly with the egg white and a little strained orange juice to a coating consistency.
2 Add a little orange colouring to make the icing a pale orange.

To assemble:
1 Split the cake through twice. Spread each layer with apricot jam and half the filling and sandwich together.
2 Lightly spread the sides of the cake with icing and cover with desiccated coconut.
3 Swirl the remaining icing on top and decorate with pieces of orange slices and angelica.

Walnut gateau

Cake:
4oz (100g) butter
4oz (100g) caster sugar
2 eggs
4½oz (115g) self-raising
flour
2 tablespoons water

Filling:
½ pint (3dl) double cream
1 level teaspoon sugar
2oz (50g) chopped walnuts

Icing and decoration:
6oz (175g) caster sugar
2 tablespoons water
1 egg white
walnuts

Cake:
1 Heat the oven Gas Mark 4; 350°F (180°C) and have ready a greased sandwich tin, 8 inches (20cm) in diameter.
2 Follow the method for making and baking the cake for Grapefruit Gateau (see page 92).

Filling:
1 Whisk the cream steadily with the sugar until it holds its shape. Stir in the chopped walnuts.
2 Split the cake through twice and sandwich together with the cream.

Icing and decoration:
1 Mix the sugar, water and egg white together in a double boiler or in a basin over hot water. Stir until the sugar dissolves.
2 Whisk with a hand electric or rotary whisk until the mixture stands in peaks.
3 Swirl over the cake and decorate with walnut halves.

Strawberry meringue gateau

(Illustrated on page 83)

Cake:
2oz (50g) butter
4oz (100g) caster sugar
4 egg yolks
4oz (100g) self-raising
flour
5 tablespoons milk

Meringue:
4 egg whites
8oz (225g) caster sugar
2oz (50g) blanched
almonds

Filling:
1lb (½ kilo) strawberries
¾ pint (4½dl) double cream
½ level tablespoon sugar

Cake:
1 Heat the oven Gas Mark 2; 300°F (150°C) and have ready two greased and lined sponge sandwich tins, 9 inches (23cm) in diameter.
2 Beat the butter and sugar together until light and creamy.
3 Beat in the egg yolks and lightly stir in the sifted flour and milk.
4 Divide the mixture between the two tins.

Meringue:
1 Whisk the egg whites until stiff, then gradually whisk in the sugar.
2 Swirl the meringue on to the sponge mixture. Chop the almonds coarsely and sprinkle on top.
3 Bake for 35 minutes. Turn carefully on to wire racks to cool.

Filling:
1 Hull and slice the strawberries, reserving a few whole ones for decoration. Sprinkle with sugar, if liked.
2 Whisk the cream and sugar together steadily till it is just creamy.
3 Sandwich the sponges together with the cream and strawberries. Decorate the top with the reserved strawberries.

Chestnut gateau

(Illustrated on page 83)

Cake:
4oz (100g) plain chocolate
15½oz (439g) can chestnut
purée
4 eggs, separated
6oz (175g) caster sugar

Filling and decoration:
2 level teaspoons Bird's
instant coffee
1 teaspoon warm water
½ pint (3dl) double cream
3oz (75g) blanched
almonds
crystallised violets

Cake:
1 Heat the oven Gas Mark 6; 400°F (200°C) and have ready two greased sandwich tins, 8 inches (20cm) in diameter. Put greased paper in the bottom of each.
2 Put the chocolate to melt on a plate over hot water. Take the chestnut purée from the can and stir well.
3 Beat the egg yolks and sugar until thick and creamy, then stir in the melted chocolate and chestnut purée.
4 Whisk the egg whites until stiff and stir lightly into the chestnut mixture.
5 Divide the mixture between the prepared tins, smooth the surface and bake for 40 minutes. Leave on a wire rack until cold.

Filling and decoration:
1 Dissolve the instant coffee in the warm water. Add to the cream and whisk steadily until it just holds its shape.
2 Use half of the coffee cream to sandwich the cakes together and swirl the rest over the top and sides.
3 Decorate with chopped browned almonds and crystallised violets.

This gateau is very moist and rather rich. It freezes well. Add the nuts and violets when completely thawed.

Black Forest gateau

(Illustrated opposite)

Cake:
4oz (100g) butter
4oz (100g) caster sugar
2 eggs
**3½oz (90g) self-raising
    flour**
½oz (15g) cocoa
1oz (25g) plain chocolate
1 tablespoon milk

Filling and decoration:
**15oz (425g) can pitted
    black cherries**
2 level teaspoons cornflour
**2 sachets Dream Topping
    and 8fl.oz (220ml) milk
    or 1 pint (6dl) double
    cream**
kirsch

Cake:
1 Heat the oven Gas Mark 4; 350°F (180°C) and have ready a greased sandwich tin, 9 inches (23cm) in diameter.
2 Beat the butter and sugar together until light and creamy.
3 Beat in the eggs, one at a time.
4 Sift the flour and cocoa together and stir lightly into the creamed mixture.
5 Dissolve the chocolate in the milk, cool, then add to the creamed mixture.
6 Turn into the prepared tin and bake in the centre of the oven for 25–30 minutes, or until springy to the touch.
7 Turn on to a wire rack to cool.

Filling:
1 Drain the black cherries and pour ¼ pint (1½dl) of the syrup on to the cornflour. Stir well.
2 Turn into a saucepan and bring to the boil, stirring all the time.
3 Add the drained cherries and leave to cool.
4 Make up the Dream Topping as directed on the packet, using the milk, or whisk the cream until it begins to thicken.

To assemble:
1 Have ready a serving plate. Split the cake through the centre and put the base on the plate. Sprinkle with kirsch.
2 Spread half the Dream Topping or whipped cream over the sponge base. Carefully spoon over most of the cherries in the syrup.
3 Place the other half of the cake on top. Sprinkle with kirsch and decorate with the remaining Dream Topping or cream, and cherries.

Frangipan tartlets

(Illustrated on page 83)
Makes 12

Pastry and filling:
**4oz (100g) sweet flan
    pastry (see page 24)**
4oz (100g) butter
4oz (100g) caster sugar
2 eggs
4oz (100g) ground almonds
1oz (25g) plain flour
little almond essence

Decoration:
6oz (175g) icing sugar
1–2 tablespoons milk
glacé cherries
angelica

Pastry and filling:
1 Heat the oven Gas Mark 5; 375°F (190°C) and have ready 12 tartlet tins, 2–3 inches (5–7cm) in diameter.
2 Use the pastry to line the tartlet tins. Prick well.
3 Beat the butter and sugar together until light and creamy. Beat in the eggs.
4 Stir in the ground almonds and sifted flour, adding a few drops of almond essence.
5 Divide the mixture between the tins and bake for about 15–20 minutes, or until golden brown and firm to the touch.
6 Remove the tartlets from the tins and leave to cool on a wire rack.

Decoration:
1 Sift the icing sugar and mix to a thick coating consistency with milk. Use to ice the tartlets.
2 Decorate with glacé cherries and angelica.

Black Forest gateau

Dacquoise

Serves 6–8

Meringue:
3 egg whites
6oz (175g) caster sugar
pinch of cream of tartar
2oz (50g) ground almonds

Filling:
½ pint (3dl) double cream
¼ pint (1½dl) thick apricot
   purée
sugar or lemon juice
   (optional)

Decoration:
icing sugar
chocolate vermicelli

Meringue:
1 Heat the oven Gas Mark 1; 275°F (140°C) and line two baking sheets with oiled greaseproof paper or foil.
2 Whisk the egg whites until stiff, add half the sugar, the cream of tartar and whisk again until stiff.
3 Fold in the remaining sugar and ground almonds.
4 Divide the mixture between the two baking sheets and form rounds, 7 inches (18cm) in diameter.
5 Bake for about 1 hour. If the paper peels away easily, the almond meringues are ready. Leave to cool.

Filling:
1 Whisk the cream steadily until it holds its shape. Reserve some for decoration and stir the rest into the apricot purée.
2 Check the flavour and add sugar or lemon juice if necessary.

To assemble:
1 Sandwich the two discs together with the apricot filling, 30–45 minutes before required.
2 Dust the top with sifted icing sugar. Decorate with the reserved cream and chocolate vermicelli.

Glacé fruit gateau

Cake:
8oz (225g) butter
8oz (225g) caster sugar
4 eggs
8oz (225g) self-raising
flour

Filling:
1 sachet Dream Topping
and 4fl.oz (110ml) milk
or ½ pint (3dl) double
cream and ½oz (15g)
caster sugar
apricot jam

Icing and decoration:
1lb (450g) sugar
¼ pint (1½dl) water
2 egg whites
glacé fruits

Cake:
1 Heat the oven Gas Mark 4; 350°F (180°C) and have ready two greased sandwich tins, 9 inches (23cm) in diameter.
2 Beat the butter and sugar together until light and creamy.
3 Add the eggs alternately with the sifted flour, beating well between each addition.
4 Add a little water if necessary to give a soft dropping consistency.
5 Divide the mixture between the two prepared tins and bake for about 30 minutes, or until springy to the touch.
6 Turn on to wire racks and leave to cool.

Filling:
1 Make up the Dream Topping as directed on the packet, using the milk, or whisk the cream with the sugar until it begins to thicken.
2 Split the cakes through the centre and sandwich together with apricot jam and Dream Topping or whipped cream. Sandwich the two cakes together with apricot jam.

Icing and decoration:
1 Brush the cake free from crumbs and put on a wire rack.
2 Put the sugar and water into a saucepan and heat gently until the sugar has completely dissolved.
3 Bring to the boil, put the lid on the saucepan and boil for 2 minutes to dissolve any sugar crystals on the sides of the saucepan.
4 Remove the lid and boil steadily to 240°F (116°C). Remove the saucepan from the heat and leave until all the bubbles subside.
5 Whisk the egg whites until stiff.
6 Pour the syrup in a thin stream on to the egg whites, whisking all the time. Continue whisking until the icing will hold soft peaks and is of a coating consistency.
7 Pour at once over the cake, then decorate the top with glacé fruits.

The icing used for this gateau is American frosting. To make it successfully you need a sugar boiling thermo-meter and a hand electric whisk. It can be done with a wire whisk but you need patience and a strong wrist.

Sponge gateau

Cake:
1½oz (40g) butter
3oz (75g) caster sugar
3 eggs
3oz (75g) self-raising flour

Icing:
4oz (100g) butter
6oz (175g) icing sugar
2 level teaspoons Bird's
  instant coffee
1 teaspoon water
red colouring

Filling and decoration:
apricot jam
blanched almonds

Cake:
1 Heat the oven Gas Mark 5; 375°F (190°C) and have ready a greased and floured sandwich tin, 8 inches (20cm) in diameter.
2 Follow the method for making the cake for Glacé Fruit Gateau (see previous recipe).
3 Turn the mixture into the prepared tin and bake in the centre of the oven for about 20 minutes.
4 Turn on to a wire rack to cool.

Icing:
1 Beat the butter until light and creamy, then gradually beat in the sifted icing sugar.
2 Divide the butter icing between two small basins.
3 Colour one with coffee by dissolving the instant coffee in the water and working in sufficient to colour and flavour the icing.
4 Colour the rest of the icing pink.

To assemble:
1 Split the cake and sandwich together with apricot jam.
2 Spread the sides of the cake with apricot jam and cover with split blanched almonds.
3 Put the cake on a serving plate, spread the top with some of the butter icing and mark into quarters.
4 Using the coffee and pink butter icing, pipe alternate quarters with small stars, keeping them close together so that the base icing is not visible.

Simple gateau

Cake:
1½oz (40g) butter
3oz (75g) caster sugar
3 eggs
3oz (75g) self-raising flour

Filling:
¼ pint (1½dl) double cream
1 level teaspoon sugar

Icing:
8oz (225g) icing sugar
milk to mix

Cake:
1 Heat the oven Gas Mark 5; 375°F (190°C) and have ready a greased and floured sandwich tin, 8 inches (20cm) in diameter.
2 Follow the directions for making the cake for Glacé Fruit Gateau (see opposite page).
3 Turn the mixture into the prepared tin and bake in the centre of the oven for about 20 minutes.
4 Turn on to a wire rack to cool.

Filling:
1 Whisk the cream steadily with the sugar until it holds its shape.

Icing:
1 Sift the icing sugar into a basin.
2 Mix to a stiff coating consistency with a little milk.

To assemble:
1 Split the sponge cake and sandwich with the sweetened whipped cream.
2 Ice completely with white icing and leave to set.
3 Decorate as liked.

Diana's gateau

4 egg whites
8oz (225g) caster sugar
4oz (100g) plain chocolate
1 pint (6dl) double cream

1 Heat the oven and leave it as low as possible.
2 Have ready two baking sheets lined with lightly oiled foil or greaseproof paper.
3 Whisk the egg whites until stiff, then gradually whisk in the sugar. Form the meringue into a disc 7 inches (18cm) in diameter on each of the prepared baking sheets.
4 Leave to dry in the oven for 3–4 hours.
5 Put the chocolate on a plate and melt gently over hot water.
6 Whisk the cream until it just starts to thicken, add the melted chocolate and continue whisking until it just holds its shape.
7 Sandwich the meringues together with a third of the cream. Swirl a further third on top and pipe the rest to decorate the gateau.

The meringue discs can be made well ahead of time and stored in an airtight tin. Assemble the gateau about 30 minutes before it is to be served to give the cream just time to meld to the meringues and make it easy to serve.

Mocha gateau

Cake:
4oz (100g) butter
4oz (100g) caster sugar
2 eggs
3½oz (90g) self-raising flour
½oz (15g) cocoa
3 level teaspoons Bird's instant coffee
1 tablespoon milk

Filling and icing:
3oz (75g) sugar
4 tablespoons water
2 egg yolks
6oz (175g) butter
1oz (25g) plain chocolate
2 level teaspoons Bird's instant coffee

Decoration:
chopped walnuts
blanched almonds

Cake:
1 Heat the oven Gas Mark 4; 350°F (180°C) and have ready a greased deep sandwich tin, 8 inches (20cm) in diameter.
2 Follow the method for making the cake for Black Forest Gateau (see page 86) but dissolve the instant coffee in place of the chocolate in the milk.
3 Turn into the prepared tin and bake in the centre of the oven for about 35 minutes, or until springy to the touch.
4 Turn on to a wire rack to cool.

Filling and icing:
1 Dissolve the sugar in the water over a very gentle heat.
2 When completely dissolved, bring to the boil and boil to 220°F (105°C).
3 Pour the syrup on to the egg yolks and whisk till thick and creamy.
4 Cream the butter and gradually beat in the cooled egg mixture.
5 Melt the chocolate in a small basin over hot water, then leave to cool. Stir into the butter cream with the instant coffee dissolved in a little water.

To assemble:
1 Split the cake through the centre and sandwich with a third of the butter cream.
2 Lightly spread the sides with almost half of the remaining cream and cover with chopped walnuts.
3 Swirl the top with the remaining butter cream and decorate with blanched almonds.

This gateau freezes very well. Allow 3½ hours at room temperature for it to defrost thoroughly.

Raspberry mille feuilles

Raspberry mille feuilles

(Illustrated above)

**8oz (225g) flaky pastry
   (see page 24)**
¾ pint (4½dl) double cream
**1lb (½ kilo) fresh
   raspberries**
icing sugar

1 Heat the oven Gas Mark 7; 425°F (220°C) and have ready two baking sheets.
2 Roll the pastry very thinly into four rounds, each 8 inches (20cm) in diameter. From the centre of one round cut a circle 4 inches (10cm) in diameter.
3 Place the pastry rounds on the baking sheets and bake for about 5 minutes, or until lightly browned and crisp. Leave to cool.
4 Gently whisk the cream, adding a little sugar, if you wish, until it just holds it shape.
5 When nearly ready to serve, assemble the gateau on a flat serving dish. Spread the three pastry layers with whipped cream. Sandwich together with raspberries, reserving a quarter of the choicest for the top.
6 Dust the pastry circle generously with sifted icing sugar and place on top. Fill the centre with the reserved raspberries.

Frozen puff pastry can be used equally well for this recipe.

Grapefruit gateau

Cake:
4oz (100g) butter
4oz (100g) caster sugar
2 eggs
4½oz (115g) self-raising
flour
2 tablespoons water

Filling:
grated rind of 2 grapefruit
3oz (75g) butter
6oz (175g) icing sugar
grapefruit juice

Icing and decoration:
8oz (225g) icing sugar
grapefruit segments
crystallised violets

Cake:
1 Heat the oven Gas Mark 4; 350°F (180°C) and have ready a greased sandwich tin, 8 inches (20cm) in diameter.
2 Beat the butter and sugar together until light and creamy.
3 Beat in the eggs, one at a time, adding a little of the sifted flour between each addition.
4 Lightly stir in the rest of the flour, adding the water to give a soft dropping consistency.
5 Turn the mixture into the prepared tin and bake in the centre of the oven for 25–30 minutes, or until well risen, golden brown and springy to the touch.
6 Turn on to a wire rack to cool.

Filling:
1 Add the grated grapefruit rind to the butter and beat well.
2 Beat in the sifted icing sugar until light and creamy.
3 Add sufficient grapefruit juice to make it light and fluffy.

Icing:
1 Sift the icing sugar and mix to a stiff coating consistency with grapefruit juice.

To assemble:
1 Split the cake in two and sandwich together with the grapefruit filling.
2 Ice the cake with the grapefruit flavoured icing.
3 For the decoration, peel the grapefruit thickly to remove all the pith and expose the flesh. With a sharp knife, cut out the segments leaving the skin behind. Decorate the cake with the grapefruit segments and crystallised violets.

The tartness of the grapefruit makes this a very refreshing gateau.

Vacherin of fruit

2 egg whites
4oz (100g) caster sugar
½ pint (3dl) double cream
fresh fruit

1 Heat the oven and leave it as low as possible. Have ready a baking sheet lined with lightly oiled foil or greaseproof paper.
2 Whisk the egg whites until stiff, then gradually whisk in the sugar. Use two thirds of the meringue to form a disc 8 inches (20cm) in diameter on the prepared baking sheet.
3 Pipe the remaining meringue in stars on the edge of the disc to form a small wall.
4 Leave to dry in the oven for about 2 hours.
5 When ready to serve, fill with whipped cream and fruit.

St. Clement's gateau

Pastry base:
4oz (100g) sweet flan
  pastry (see page 24)

Cake:
4oz (100g) butter
4oz (100g) caster sugar
grated rind of 1 orange
2 eggs
4½oz (115g) self-raising
  flour
2 tablespoons orange juice

Filling and icing:
½ pint (3dl) double cream
2 level teaspoons caster
  sugar
8oz (225g) icing sugar
lemon juice

Decoration:
lemon curd
¼ pint (1½dl) double cream
1 level teaspoon caster
  sugar
crystallised orange and
  lemon slices

Pastry base:
1 Heat the oven Gas Mark 5; 375°F (190°C) and have ready a sandwich tin, 9 inches (23cm) in diameter.
2 Roll the sweet flan pastry to a circle to fit into the base of the tin.
3 Bake in the centre of the oven for 25–30 minutes.

Cake:
1 Reduce the oven temperature to Gas Mark 4; 350°F (180°C) and have ready a greased sandwich tin, 9 inches (23cm) in diameter.
2 Follow the method for making the cake for Grapefruit Gateau (see opposite page) but add the grated rind of the orange to the creamed mixture and use 2 tablespoons orange juice in place of the water.
3 Turn the mixture into the prepared tin and bake in the centre of the oven for 30–35 minutes.

Filling and icing:
1 Whisk the cream steadily with the sugar until it holds its shape.
2 Sift the icing sugar into a basin and mix to a stiff coating consistency with lemon juice.

To assemble:
1 Split the cake and sandwich together with sweetened whipped cream.
2 Sandwich the cake to the pastry base with lemon curd.
3 Ice the cake with lemon glacé icing and decorate with rosettes of sweetened whipped cream and crystallised orange and lemon slices.

Chocolate and coffee gateau

Cake:
3 eggs, separated
3oz (75g) caster sugar
2 level teaspoons Bird's
  instant coffee
2 teaspoons warm water
3oz (75g) self-raising flour

Filling and icing:
3oz (75g) sugar
4 tablespoons water
2 egg yolks
6oz (175g) butter
2oz (50g) plain chocolate

Decoration:
3oz (75g) hazelnuts

Cake:
1 Heat the oven Gas Mark 6; 400°F (200°C) and have ready a greased and lined Swiss roll tin, about 9 inches by 12 inches (23cm by 30cm).
2 Whisk the egg whites stiffly, then gradually whisk in the sugar. Continue beating until the mixture is stiff.
3 Beat in the egg yolks. Dissolve the coffee in the warm water and stir carefully into the mixture.
4 Very lightly fold in the sifted flour. Turn the mixture into the prepared tin and bake towards the top of the oven for 12 minutes.
5 Turn on to a wire rack to cool.

Filling and icing:
Follow the method for Mocha Gateau (see page 90) but omit the instant coffee and use 2oz (50g) chocolate.

To assemble:
1 Cut the sponge into three and layer together with some of the chocolate cream.
2 Spread a little on the sides and coat with chopped hazelnuts.
3 Decorate the top with the remaining chocolate cream and hazelnuts.

Index